The Ownership Quotient

The Ownership Quotient

Putting the Service Profit Chain to Work for Unbeatable Competitive Advantage

James L. Heskett

W. Earl Sasser

Joe Wheeler

Harvard Business Press

Boston, Massachusetts

Library of congress Cataloging-in-publication Data

Heskett, James L.
    The ownership quotient: putting the service profit chain to work for unbeatable competitive advantage / James L. Heskett, W. Earl Sasser, Joe Wheeler.
        p.   cm.
    ISBN 978-1-4221-1023-2
    1. Word-of-mouth advertising.   2. Customer services.   3. Employee ownership.
I. Sasser, Earl W.   II. Wheeler, Joe.   III. Title.
    HF5827.95.H47 2008
    659.1—dc22

                                                                              2008022313

CONTENTS

1

Introduction

Lanham Napier is CEO of Rackspace Hosting, based in San Antonio, Texas. Napier is obsessed with the development of customer owners, even though he doesn't use the term. His organization, which provides IT hosting services for its business customers, makes surprisingly high profits in a commoditized business that many regard as operating in the gritty backwater of the Internet.

Rackspace succeeds by carefully selecting its customers, providing them with easy access to its customer-centered teams as well as personalized, fast responses to their needs, and listening to and acting on their reactions and suggestions. The results are impressive customer satisfaction and loyalty levels, referral rates that account for a high proportion of Rackspace's new business, low marketing costs that help deliver relatively high margins, and annual business growth rates of just under 60 percent from 2003 to 2007—in spite of prices that can sometimes be higher than competitors'.

In the explanation we heard repeatedly from Rackspace executives, "Customers act as if they own the company." They show intense loyalty, commitment, and engagement and even take responsibility for the success of Rackspace's business—the true mark of ownership. And as you will see, none of this could have happened without a strong sense of ownership among "Rackers," the company's term for its employees.

We explore the lessons from Rackspace and many other ownership-oriented organizations throughout this book. But the bottom line is that a customer who behaves like an owner is worth more than a hundred typical price-sensitive customers over the customer owner's lifetime with your organization. Similarly, the lifetime value of an employee who can promote customer ownership is priceless. And an organization that learns how to cultivate an ownership attitude creates a self-reinforcing relationship between customers and frontline employees.

A customer owner is one who tries a product or service, is so satisfied that she returns to buy more, states a willingness to tell others of her experiences, actually convinces others to buy, provides constructive criticism of existing offerings, and even suggests or helps test new products or ideas. Some customer owners even help select new employees.

Employee owners take satisfaction in creating value for customers. They exhibit their sense of ownership through loyalty, referrals of other high-potential employees to the organization, and suggestions for improving the quality of processes and work life as well as the organization's overall effectiveness in serving customers. Employee owners are the most important contributors to a company's customer ownership quotient—or OQ—which we define as the proportion of all customers who are actively engaged in significant work on behalf of a product, service, or brand. Similarly, the employee OQ is the proportion of all employees who are so satisfied, loyal, and committed to the value offered by the organization that they contribute ideas for further improvement and help recruit high-potential friends to join the cause.

These descriptions use the term *ownership* not in a financial sense but in the sense of commitment to shared values and desired outcomes. But when companies learn to engineer ownership, everyone also gains financially because a strong community of owners creates a larger pie to divide among employees, customers, investors, and other partners.

Who are these potential customer and employee owners? How can you identify them? How can you expand their ranks and nurture their sense of ownership? How can you track the results of your efforts? Which companies are leading the way, and what can the rest of us learn from them? These are our concerns in this book. But first, a few words about how we arrived at these questions and their answers.

ADVANCING THE CONCEPT OF THE SERVICE PROFIT CHAIN

Rackspace's accomplishments exemplify the best of next-generation thinking about the service profit chain, a set of insights that we have been examining for more than twenty years. (For more on this, see "The Service Profit Chain: A Two-Minute Primer.") In its simplest form, the service profit chain is about developing a working environment in which carefully selected, highly capable, engaged employees interact with customers to create customer value far superior to that offered by the competition.

As a result of careful application of service profit chain thinking, customers remain loyal (exhibiting high rates of retention), they buy more (related sales), they tell others about their positive experience (providing referrals), and they suggest ways of enhancing the customer experience by complaining constructively, suggesting new products or services and process improvements (research and development). These "four R's" fuel long-term profitability and organic growth. They also spawn new ideas that lead directly to new business development that delivers the results that customers really seek.

In formulating and refining these concepts originally, we learned a great deal from a group of pioneering firms such as USAA, MBNA, Intuit, and Southwest Airlines. They taught us the clear relationships that exist between employee satisfaction and loyalty and customer satisfaction and loyalty, as well as the impact that these factors can have on growth and profitability. Although our original research partners didn't have a name for these phenomena, we came to regard them as forming a service profit chain. Other academics, consultants, and business executives added to the evidence of the validity of the model. Some established

The Service Profit Chain: A Two-Minute Primer

When we introduced the service profit chain in the early 1990s, we described seven fundamental propositions that formed the links in the chain:

1. **Customer loyalty drives profitability and growth.** A 5 percent increase in customer loyalty can boost profits by 25 to 85 percent. The benefit of retaining customers on average one more year has a significant impact on the bottom line.

2. **Customer satisfaction drives customer loyalty.** This was a new idea in the beginning, but now we find few organizations that are not focused on driving improvement in their *top-box* customer satisfaction scores (the highest ratings given by those surveyed) precisely for this reason.

3. **Value drives customer satisfaction.** *Value*—results plus process quality in relation to total cost to the customer—is critical in creating satisfied customers.

4. **Employee capability (latitude within limits to deliver value to targeted customers) and productivity drive value.**

causal relationships—for example, that the chain is forged most logically beginning with employees—whereas earlier, only correlations between elements of the chain had been measured.[1] Since then, hundreds of organizations around the world have used the service profit chain as a business model for achieving improved performance. They now constitute a laboratory for observation that we have studied for this book.

This time around we engaged a recent set of adopters (see "A Note About the Research") that were advancing the application of the service profit chain as a performance and growth platform. It became clear to us that some of these organizations, armed with sophisticated emerging information technology, had taken our ideas further than any of us had envisioned. They had, in a sense, developed more scientific ways of

5. **Employee loyalty drives productivity.** Service profit chain leaders draw a clear line of sight between the impact of lower turnover on the productivity of the operating model. Having loyal employees also means that you spend less money recruiting and training new employees, and in high-service organizations those savings can be significant.

6. **Quality of work life drives employee satisfaction and loyalty.** Quality of work life includes such things as the fairness of one's boss, the chance to work with "winners," the opportunity for personal development, and reasonable compensation. In addition, the capability (latitude within limits) of frontline employees to produce results for valued customers remains an essential driver of employee satisfaction, retention, and productivity.

7. **Value delivered (as perceived by customers) in relation to cost yields long-term profit.**

Note: For additional information about the service profit chain, see James L. Heskett, W. Earl Sasser Jr., and Leonard A. Schlesinger, *The Service Profit Chain* (New York: The Free Press, 1997); and James L. Heskett et al., "Putting the Service Profit Chain to Work," *Harvard Business Review,* March–April 1994.

thinking about them. They were using powerful new techniques to deliver value to employees and customers and, through them, to shareholders as well.

Across the board, we found that these service profit chain leaders have worked to align key components of their businesses—marketing, operations, information, and human resources—into a single force, dedicated to consistently exceeding their customers' expectations at critical moments of truth.[2] They have created strategies, policies, and practices that integrate logic and technology to support the people who deliver value for customers. Most important, they have set out to create a core of employees and customers that we have come to think of as owners.

A Note About the Research

We began by conducting an extensive literature search of research and case studies that tested and demonstrated the impact of the service profit chain over the past fifteen years. This work included revisiting case studies we had written on organizations such as the New York Police Department and ING Direct, but for the most part, we decided not to revisit organizations such as USAA and Southwest Airlines, about which we have written extensively elsewhere. We then selected a core sample of companies that had been recognized for accomplishments such as high customer satisfaction, best places to work, or significant market share, assuming that these were organizations that could demonstrate best practice on two or more links in the service profit chain. To these we added several other companies about which we learned, in some cases through direct interviews, during our study:

Baptist Health Care	Build-A-Bear Workshop®
Fairmont Hotels & Resorts	Harrah's Entertainment
ING Direct	Irving Oil Ltd.
PrairieStone Pharmacy	Rackspace Hosting
SAS	Victoria's Secret
Wegmans Food Markets	EMC

For more information on this research, please visit our Web site at www.ownershipquotient.com.

BEYOND SATISFACTION AND LOYALTY: THE OWNERSHIP QUOTIENT

Every company that adopts the concepts of the service profit chain tries to create the conditions that foster high rates of satisfaction and loyalty among employees and customers. These are preconditions for ownership.

Figure 1-1 depicts what we call the *ownership hierarchy*. It shows that owners are satisfied, loyal, and engaged or committed (willing to recommend an organization or its products and services to others). Beyond

FIGURE 1-1

The ownership hierarchy (for employees and customers)

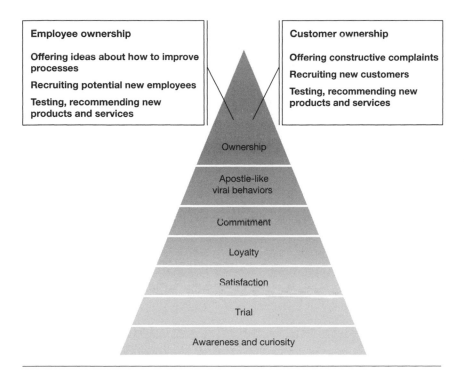

that, they act as apostles, recruiting new customers and employees. As customers, they are in frequent contact with the company, constructively complaining or suggesting improvements in products, processes, or services. They help in testing new products or services. They may, at times, be a pain in the neck, but they may also be the source of useful new product ideas.

Measurable indicators that your organization has a high customer OQ go beyond high customer curiosity, satisfaction, loyalty, and commitment to highlight such things as:

- A high proportion of new customers resulting from referrals

- A significant proportion of new or improved products resulting from customer suggestions and constructive criticism

- A high degree of customer willingness to test new products and processes

The ultimate measure of ownership is the proportion of your customers actively engaged in significant work on behalf of the product, service, or brand. You can determine this by asking them whether the following apply.

- They have made referrals to potential customers.

- Those referrals were successful.

- They have helped test a product or service.

- They have provided constructive complaints regarding existing products or services.

- They have suggested process, product, or service improvements.

The core number of customer owners need not be large. Companies with ownership quotients as small as 3 percent have achieved significant success. But the greater the ownership quotient, the higher the probability that your organization will distance itself from its competition, in extreme examples literally changing the rules of the game for entire industries, as companies such as Toyota, eBay, Intuit, Southwest Airlines, and Amazon.com have done.

The primary driver of customer ownership is the employee ownership quotient. It is measured by determining the proportion of employees who have in, say, the past year, done any of the following:

- Succeeded in persuading a friend or acquaintance to apply for work at the organization

- In some way constructively criticized the ways things are done

- Offered a suggestion for a process change or product improvement

- Volunteered to test new processes or products

Another measure of the employee OQ is the proportion of applicants or new hires that results from employee recommendations

Because it takes a significant, sustained effort from all employees—but especially those in direct contact with customers—the employee OQ must be several times that of the customer OQ you wish to sustain. In fact, the ideal target level for the employee OQ should approach 100 percent.

A high employee OQ enhances value for customers through increased retention and continuity in customer relations. It also dramatically reduces the costs of hiring, training, and lost productivity from turnover. It helps explain why service organizations such as Rackspace and Harrah's Entertainment deliver high value for customers at relatively modest costs.

BUILDING THE OQ: HARRAH'S ENTERTAINMENT

Perhaps the most advanced of our research sites in engineering ownership is Harrah's Entertainment, the Las Vegas based gaming empire that includes Harrah's, Golden Horseshoe, and Caesars Palace. The company's remarkable database yields astonishing results that underscore the importance of the ownership quotient. But it took a concerted effort to push Harrah's beyond the original benefits of the service profit chain. Let's explore a bit of that history.

In 1987, Laughlin, Nevada, appeared to be the ideal location to open a new Harrah's casino and resort hotel. A resort town in the southern-most tip of Nevada, Laughlin had transformed a piece of the rugged Mojave Desert into a fast-growing tourist destination. By the late 1990s, revenues at Harrah's Laughlin had grown, and its customer satisfaction scores were the envy of the rest of the company. Life in Laughlin was good—until things changed.

By 1999, Laughlin began to face stiff competition from Native American gaming in Southern California and Arizona. Although revenues had not fallen off, they had flattened considerably from previous years. Mirroring the revenue performance, customer satisfaction scores also had leveled off, triggering a falloff in bonuses keyed to improvement in the satisfaction scores. For the previous two quarters, employees had received no bonuses despite being the highest-scoring property in the company, with 55 percent top-box customer expressions of satisfaction.

John Koster, the new general manager of the property, commented, "There was a belief by many of our staff in Laughlin at that point that we had gone as far as we were going to be able to go. I didn't think we had reached that point. I could quote example after example of employees not returning my 'hellos,' avoiding eye contact. We had to take an aggressive stance on holding our staff accountable for the service behaviors that they were supposed to be embracing."

Koster also found supervisors who were hung up on "administrivia." They were not training their subordinates in prescribed customer relations behaviors and were not holding people accountable. Koster convinced John Bruns, the corporate vice president of customer satisfaction assurance, to validate the most important service behaviors driving top-box customer satisfaction, with the goal of getting every guest-contact department to exceed customer expectations for each behavior.

Next, to combat Laughlin's sliding market share, Koster decided to bring a larger market directly to Laughlin. He used Harrah's customer relationship management (CRM) system to identify the most valuable (high theoretical value per trip guests) customers from a Total Rewards loyalty database of more than 40 million customers segmented by geography to suggest who would respond favorably to an offer to spend a complimentary weekend getaway expressly at Harrah's Laughlin. Following this targeted direct marketing experiment, he expanded Laughlin's air charter program to about three hundred flights per year and began flying in targeted customers ("Diamonds") from cities around the United States.

To ensure that the Laughlin casino captured as much of the potential gaming dollar as possible from these most profitable Diamond customers, Koster's team redesigned the arrival and departure experience. First, the casino bought new buses and met customers at the airport rather than run the risk that customers might rent autos and stop at other casinos on their way to Harrah's. Then the Laughlin team redesigned processes for interacting with guests. After being welcomed and engaged by the bus driver, customers watch an information video en route to the casino. As the bus pulls into the property, guests encounter a party atmosphere day or night, including music, drinks, and an opportunity to have a picture taken with a showgirl. To banish the need for customers to wait at the registration counter, their room key packets are ready upon arrival.

Koster reports on the impact of these changes: "You would see many tired travelers suddenly perk up and get in the spirit of a true vacation. Instead of heading to bed they headed to the restaurants, bars, and casino to enjoy themselves."

At the casino, Harrah's data-driven program delivers customized service at each of several touch points. For example, when a Diamond customer on slot machine 387 signals for service, a Harrah's associate is able to ask, "The usual, Mr. Smith?" and then track the time it takes for a server to fill Mr. Smith's request. It's the kind of individual attention the customer can't get at the casino across the street. At the end of Mr. Smith's memorable experience, he receives photographs of his arrival as a trip memento.

Not content with those improvements, management continued training Laughlin's frontline associates to reinforce the five service behaviors most important to customer delight: friendly greeting, smiling and eye contact, upbeat and positive attitude, checking for guest satisfaction, and a warm farewell. Managers also focused on reducing or eliminating the wait time for Diamond customers during specific parts of the experience, such as dining, valet parking, and the cashier station.

After twenty-one months without improvement in top-box scores, the fourth quarter of 2003 saw employees begin to meet their targets again. They increased the satisfaction score to 57.2 percent. After finishing all of the training, in the second quarter of 2004 they broke the 60 percent barrier, something no other Harrah's property had ever done. During the next quarter they improved to 62 percent, and in the last quarter of 2004 they achieved 64.2 percent. In addition, associates were removed (or removed themselves) from customer-facing roles in which they were not capable of delighting guests. This included supervisors who could not meet the requirements of the revised position descriptions, which defined their roles as being on the floor 85 to 90 percent of the time engaging with guests and training and coaching employees.

In less than fifteen months' time, customer satisfaction scores rose by eight percentage points, an increase that was unheard-of at Harrah's. Bonuses once again flowed. And the success continued to feed on itself, so much so that Harrah's doubled its growth in earnings before interest, taxes, depreciation, and amortization (EBITDA) in only three years.

What are the lessons from Harrah's Laughlin? Is it a leadership turn-around story? A customer service story? A customer relations management story? It's all of those. But it also illustrates the carefully managed ways in which an organization enlisted its best customers—those most likely to think of themselves as owners—to help turn around a flagging operating unit. To do so, it instituted practices on the ground that helped its employees become winners and owners as well. By early 2008, the company had pushed the lessons from Laughlin to a new level, using detailed information and insights from its Total Rewards customer affinity program, as you will see later.

If an impressive OQ adds so much value, why haven't measures and responses such as those developed at Harrah's gained widespread use? There are several reasons. One is that management in most companies simply hasn't been ready to make these changes. It has taken some time for corporate leaders to accept the idea that customer attitudes and behaviors are a mirror reflection of, and are driven by, employee attitudes and behaviors, and that useful change begins within the organization. We are just reaching the point where management has become interested in measuring and acting upon customer commitment (willingness to recommend) more than merely customer satisfaction. It's easier, less complex, and very tempting to measure satisfaction or commitment by using one or two questions. But it is not clear how effective these measures are, by themselves, in predicting future growth and profitability.

Technology—particularly in assembling, mining, storing, and communicating information—makes it eminently possible to measure the OQ of customers and employees, link it to long-term performance, and then carry out the experiments and activities that will increase OQ value over time—to the delight of employees, customers, and investors alike.

How many owners does your organization have? What proportion of the total do they represent? How do you know? What are you doing to develop the cadre of owners?

THE PLAN OF THIS BOOK

Seasoned service profit chain leaders such as Harrah's view their OQ-building efforts as closer to a science than a craft. Think of the OQ as both a measure of the effectiveness of policies and practices that enhance value for customers and employees and a predictor of future organizational performance. In the chapters that follow we'll concentrate on selected policies, practices, and measures employed by organizations likely to be found at the head of rankings in both customer satisfaction and as good places to work. Our purpose is to help you find your own combination of ingredients that will work best for your organization. In the chapters that follow, we'll help you see how you can do just that.

Increasing your ownership quotients starts with developing a strategy that delivers differentiated, customized value to customers and employees, our concern in chapter 2. For example, the management of ING Direct, the world's fastest-growing thrift organization, has designed experiences based on a vision that provides compelling value for its targeted customers and employees. At the core is an intent and capability to deliver customer and employee experiences that exceed expectations at critical moments of truth that each truly values. These expectations are centered on results (rather than products or services) and provide a focal point for everything from business definition to policies and practices to growth through business development that extends and enhances the value you deliver.

Chapter 3 explores how to leverage value over cost. Customized offerings often carry a higher value for customers, but they don't need to cost more. That's where value levers come in. They take many forms. For example, at PrairieStone Pharmacy, an innovative chain of retail pharmacies, levers range from the redefinition of the job of pharmacist to unique applications of technology. Rackspace Hosting achieves leverage through its unique customer-centered, team-based organization and distinctive Racker culture, all supported by a common technological base.

Chapter 4 helps you think about how you can put customers to work. Many customers are more than happy to put themselves to work for their favorite brands. A company that invites customers to help create the kinds of value they desire is offering them the opportunity to control some aspects of their purchase. With that control comes the chance to customize the aspects they value most, and with that chance comes an expanded sense of ownership. From involving hernia patients in their own recovery at Toronto's Shouldice Hospital to creating an online community for frequent business travelers at InterContinental Hotels, the possibilities for putting customers to work are limited only by the imagination.

Chapter 5, "Boost Your Employee OQ," discusses the ways you can foster value and a sense of ownership for employees. Your customer OQ is a function of your employee OQ. Beyond satisfaction, loyalty, and commitment, employee owners experience real pleasure in their ability to deliver value for customers. They offer suggestions for improving the business and making it a better place to work, and they identify and recruit other high-potential employees.

How do you boost the sense of ownership for employees? The companies in our sample do so by learning to create the kinds of value that matter most to employees. Not surprisingly, financial compensation represents only one aspect of the value employees seek. Recognizing this, companies such as Baptist Health Care, Fairmont Hotels & Resorts, Wegmans Food Markets, and SAS create what we call a *cycle of capability*: a self-reinforcing set of activities that helps employees feel like winners when they deliver winning results for customers.

Chapter 6, "Engineer Ownership Through Anticipatory Management," describes how Harrah's Entertainment, Build-A-Bear Workshop, and other organizations are taking the concepts of the service profit chain to a new level. Business literature is filled with reports of companies investing heavily in CRM, data warehousing, direct marketing, supply chain management, and other enterprise-wide systems to improve almost any business metric one can imagine. Your own organization may have implemented some of them or may be considering such efforts. But true customer delight often results from the creation of "one enterprise" centered on employees and customers, operating from a common base of extensive information about customer behaviors and organization capabilities, with functions working side by side and encouraged by multifunctional team incentives to achieve coordinated solutions. The goal is to address employee and customer needs before they arise—a kind of anticipatory management—rather than merely react to them.

Chapter 7, "Build a Strong and Adaptive Ownership Culture," explores how leading service organizations are doing just that. Baptist Health Care, Irving Oil, and SAS, among others, are developing much more than a loyal customer base. They are enlisting a community of owners among employees, customers, and suppliers from which they endeavor to obtain customer referrals, constructive complaints, and suggestions for new products and services as well as ways to help improve the business. These organizations know the power of creating such an ownership culture and community. They know how little it costs to do so. And they recognize the value of their investments in sustaining the gains in profit and growth. Finally, in chapter 8 we examine what it takes to sustain your success as an organization that fosters ownership. Google, the company *Fortune* magazine recently identified as the best place to work in the United States, offers an inspiring example of management practices that engage employee and customer owners to help create the value that both groups desire. But can Google sustain its success? And can the OQ work for companies in less glamorous industries, even those that risk commoditization of the products and services they deliver? Cemex, the best-in-Mexico producer of cement and related products, thinks it can. So does Lanham Napier at Rackspace Hosting—and so do we. We'll tell you how and why we've come to believe in the power of the philosophy represented by the ownership quotient.

THE PAYOFF

None of the managers we studied would have shown much interest in these ideas if they were merely theoretical. Lanham Napier is a believer, not a theorist. He has estimated that a Rackspace customer exhibiting ownership behaviors is worth at least a hundred who don't. He and his team turned around his company in a very difficult industry by building a strategy centered on these ideas, as we will see later.

At Fairmont Hotels & Resorts, management has studied the relationship between employee engagement and quality of service and found that hotels with the highest employee engagement scores also have the highest guest service scores (as measured by J.D. Power surveys and Richey International benchmarking standards audits).The correlations between the two measures provide evidence that its straighforward operating philosophy, "We believe that talented and engaged Colleagues will provide memorable service and create Guest loyalty which in-turn drives profitability and long-term sustainability," is working.[3]

Fairmont's Employee Engagement Survey uses three indices to measure employee ownership: a Rational Index, an Emotional Index, and a Leadership Index. Their 2007 study revealed that all three of these engagement indices correlate to high service scores—and most interestingly, the Emotional Index has the strongest correlation of the three. The Emotional Index is made up of several survey items that examine how employees feel about various aspects of work including factors such as shared values, commitment to the organization, motivational energy, contribution to organizational success, and leadership effectiveness. It measures the "heart" and the "will" of Fairmont employees that is so critical to creating an emotional connection with their guests. Carolyn

Clark, senior vice president of human resources, told us, "We believe the emotional engagement of our Colleagues and our 'warm and engaging' style of service is one of the things that truly defines the Fairmont guest experience, setting us apart from the competition and helping us achieve our mission of 'turning moments into memories for our guests'" with higher guest satisfaction and thus provides the greatest opportunity for increasing service scores.[4] More specifically, hotels in the top 10 percent on their Emotional Index score demonstrated a 12 percent improvement in their Richey score—and better results in terms of revenue and profitability.[5]

The results at Harrah's Entertainment provide further dramatic evidence of the power of customer and employee ownership and the importance of developing and tracking it. We were particularly interested in Harrah's Entertainment because of its extensive customer database, by which it is able to estimate the potential lifetime value of millions of individual customers. Diamond, Platinum, and Gold customers have prospective lifetime values of $100,000, $20,000, and $2,000, respectively. Harrah's recently added a new category, Seven Star, for those total reward members with a yearly value of $50,000 or more.

In early 2008, when we posed questions designed to measure Harrah's OQ to a sample of each of these groups (overall, roughly forty-five hundred customers at all three gaming properties—Harrah's, Horseshoe, and Caesars), we found remarkable results.

Seven Star and Diamond customers, although registering roughly the same "willingness to recommend" levels as Gold customers, actually had made 20 percent more recommendations to friends to visit Harrah's properties than Gold customers during the preceding year.[6] Further, their recommendations were more effective, resulting in 32 percent more recruits, with an estimated total lifetime value 73 percent greater than those recruited by Gold customers.

The comparisons didn't stop there. Seven Star and Diamond customers offered more than twice as many suggestions for service improvements as Gold customers did. They were 16 percent more willing than

Gold customers to attend a gathering organized by Harrah's to identify new service ideas. And they were 39 percent more willing to help Harrah's select new frontline service employees.

As defined by Harrah's management, Seven Star and Diamond customers have lifetime values at least fifty times those of Gold customers. Perhaps most remarkable of all, we found that as a group the Seven Star and Diamond customers attracted, *in only the twelve months preceding the study*, a new group of customers whose aggregate lifetime value is greater than their own. And that figure includes only those new recruits that Harrah's was able to identify. It helps explain why only the 8 percent of Harrah's customers who behave like owners (comprising its customer OQ) have a profound impact on its profits.

None of this would have been possible without a high rate of ownership among Harrah's employees. We found, in a companion survey, that 54 percent of employees had recommended Harrah's as a place to work to two or more of their friends.

Does the ownership quotient pay off? You be the judge. In late 2006, Harrah's board of directors accepted an offer from two private equity firms to acquire the company for a price representing a threefold increase in enterprise value over a five-year period.

If Harrah's and other high-OQ organizations have found new ways to enhance their performance through the service profit chain—and we're convinced that they have—then other organizations can learn from their example. Let us turn now to what we see as the first step: building ownership into the strategic value vision.

Build Ownership into Your Strategic Value Vision

A strong ownership quotient starts with your strategic value vision. To build a strategy that fosters ownership, you need to think systematically about questions such as these: which customers do you want to serve? What specific, customized results are you trying to deliver for them? Will your approach differentiate you from competitors? Will your customers and employees find value in the work you choose to do? And will you be able to deliver that value profitably? An organization that can answer these questions appropriately has already taken its first steps toward developing its ownership quotient.

Anticipating and exceeding the needs and wants of individual customers and employees are exciting missions. Creating a strategic value vision that outlines how to do so across an organization and in various distribution channels is even more exciting. It can change the rules of the game, especially for mature industries with entrenched management practices.

For example, how would you revitalize the stodgy savings bank?

RETHINKING THE STRATEGIC VALUE VISION OF
A SAVINGS BANK: ING DIRECT

Arkadi Kuhlmann, CEO of ING Direct, feels the pain suffered by many savers: low interest rates, high fees, and minimum balance requirements.[1] His strategic value vision offers pain relief for ING Direct's target customers. It begins with a basic question: what if a service to savers could be designed to offer extraordinarily high interest rates, no fees, and no minimums of any kind? ING Direct's parent organization, Netherlands-based ING, determined that there might be a good market for such a service, even among sophisticated investors—and a new savings bank strategy was born.

But why, in an industry several millennia old, hadn't others already started a business to relieve this kind of pain? As some of our colleagues are fond of asking, "Why was the twenty-dollar bill still on the floor? Why hadn't anyone picked it up?"

In their rush to relieve what they perceived as other kinds of pain—namely, the need for one-stop shopping—large financial institutions had added increasing numbers of products and services to their portfolios. The costs to provide these products varied; some were high, and others were low. But as banks bundled services and products, costs were merged. As offerings became more complex, costs often rose as well. Customers were offered solutions involving component products and services whose costs were averaged across the package. And in the rush to accommodate high-net-worth customers, large banking institutions often neglected those who simply wanted to build their savings.

Banking increasingly had become centered on transactions, typified by checking accounts. But transactions cost a lot of money. Banks rarely cover costs associated with checking services. So full-service banks must make it up in part by reducing the interest paid on savings. To put it simply, savings account profits are used to help subsidize checking account losses.

By avoiding checking services and concentrating on savings (and simple mortgages) at very low costs, ING Direct found that it could offer much higher interest rates on savings accounts and still make money. And by eliminating fees and minimums, the company encouraged its customers to maintain high-cost checking accounts at their existing banks while transferring funds not needed there to a savings account at ING Direct. By leveraging the efforts of dedicated, productive employees with effective support systems, the company provided highly desirable outcomes for those customers who simply desired high interest rates on savings and were willing to perform their own transactions, primarily by Internet as well as by phone and mail.

Traditional banks were not likely to mount any sort of competitive retaliation. They dismissed the idea of imitating ING Direct's model as a mistake that would only cannibalize their existing business. Further, competitors would have had to retrain customers who had been taught for years to expect a full range of services at high cost.

This attitude created a large opportunity for ING Direct. It didn't have the constraints imposed by traditional banking. The parent didn't operate banks in North America until ING Direct began operations, first in Canada and then in the United States. Within seven years after its founding in the United States in 2000, ING Direct had become the fastest-growing bank in the world and the fourth largest thrift bank in the country, with assets of $80 billion, and in 2007 it generated $395 million in pretax earnings for its parent. All this in one of the oldest and simplest businesses in the world.

ASSEMBLING THE INGREDIENTS

The ING Direct experience has a lot to teach us about the key ingredients of a strategic value vision:

- Target market focus

- Value for customers (based on results and the quality of the experience in obtaining those results, in relation to price and access costs)

- Operating leverage

- Support system excellence

Figure 2-1 diagrams how ING Direct defines these four elements for customers as well as for employees.

First comes *market focus*. ING Direct knows exactly which customers it wants to serve. More important, it has answered one of the most difficult questions in both for-profit and not-for-profit enterprise: which customers *don't* we want to serve? At ING Direct, the target market does not include customers who are most comfortable transacting business in person or by talking to someone, as opposed to transacting business over the Internet. The company doesn't operate bank branches; that would cost too much. It does offer outstanding service by phone if needed. But serving customers who need too much of this kind of service quickly becomes unprofitable. Such customers are personally and carefully coached to close their accounts in order to preserve the focus of the customer base. By early 2008, more than 10,000 customers on average were being asked personally and nicely, but firmly, to close their accounts every month. But this number was small compared with a customer base that was growing by 100,000 per month, to a total nearing 7 million.

For those customers it does target, ING Direct provides *value* —results and quality experiences in relation to cost—which is the second important element of a strategic value vision. ING Direct delivers outstanding value for its target customers: interest rates on its savings accounts typically have been as much as eight times the national average. And the service it provides to the small portion of customers who seek help is rated the highest in the industry, further boosting its customer OQ.

Third, all this is achieved through a remarkable set of policies, practices, and technologies that leverage value over costs, helping ING Direct maintain a cost basis that is roughly one-fifth that of full-service banks. ING Direct accounts are opened without face-to-face contact, thereby reducing costs significantly. But care is taken to provide high-quality personal service if it is needed. In fact, a bank that operates no branches

FIGURE 2-1

Elements of the ING Direct strategic value vision

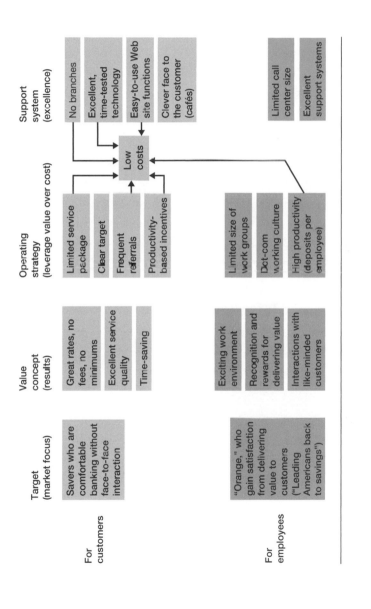

(but operates five Internet coffee shops in the United States to provide a personal "face" to the customer and garner publicity buzz) regularly scores far higher than any other U.S. banking institution on customer service. As a result, customers tell their friends about the bank, helping ING Direct further reduce its marketing costs.

ING Direct customers don't just tell others about their experiences; they recruit them just as one expects of an owner. As a result, 40 percent of all new customers come to the bank through referrals. This practice produces a customer acquisition cost of less than $100, roughly one-fourth that of the industry as a whole. This $300 savings per customer, when applied to a customer acquisition rate that recently was about a million new customers per year, yields $300 million in marketing savings per year. It has made ING Direct a veritable customer acquisition machine.

But why are there so many referrals?

The Importance of Being Orange

Referrals result from an operating strategy that begins with employees, who are selected and groomed as carefully as customers. ING Direct hires people in part for their belief in the company's crusade to lead customers back to saving, and it supports them with excellent technology as well as a carefully selected support center (not call center) organization, productivity-based incentives, and management. That's where the cycle of focus, value, leveraging, and excellence begins again, this time with employees.

ING Direct tries to make sure that all its people have an "orange" attitude, so named for the predominant color in its branding and marketing materials. "Being orange" means that you are on the side of the customer and are willing to make any effort to work more productively to enable the company to pay higher interest rates. It means that on your way to work at the company's headquarters in Wilmington, Delaware, you shake your fist at the billboard trumpeting Wilmington's other large financial service provider, a credit card issuer. Why shake your fist? It's because you regard credit cards as evil in contrast to savings. Orange people border on the fanatical in their view of the value of savings accounts for customers. This helps explain why they can be effective in encouraging ownership behaviors in customers with whom they do not have face-to-face contact.

Having hired people who are orange by nature, the company trains them to provide outstanding service, supported by state-of-the-art computer systems designed to give them maximum information to use in solving customer problems. This training and support enable employees to succeed in ways that matter to them by providing personalized, customized responses to customers in need of help.

Having been hired for attitude, trained for skills, and amply supported, employees are then ready to be given a great deal of problem-solving latitude. In fact, part of the value that support center employees obtain in working for ING Direct is the ability to deliver results to targeted customers and to be rewarded for doing so. The company's focus on creating the right internal capabilities helps explain why customer service associates achieve high customer satisfaction scores from customers who never see them. It also helps explain ING Direct's high employee OQ.

To leverage productivity, employees work and are rewarded in teams. As a result, there is little risk that they will give away the store, no matter how much latitude they are given to deliver results. And the teams are housed in support centers limited to roughly 200 to 250 employees to foster a positive working environment. When one support center is outgrown, another is created. Several are located on Wilmington's riverfront.

Teams are compensated well, in part on customer service scores and in part on their ability to reduce costs even more. And given the ING Direct operating strategy, productivity is astounding. Each employee services roughly six times the assets serviced by employees at full-service banks. The net result of this leverage is that at ING Direct, interest paid to its customers represents 86 percent of operating costs, a figure significantly higher than its competitors.

This didn't happen by chance. ING Direct is led by a CEO who is not your typical banker. A leather-jacketed motorcycle enthusiast, Arkadi Kuhlmann brings his freewheeling style to the business on a daily basis.

But beneath the exterior is someone with an infectious fanaticism about customer and employee ownership.

If you don't think that this kind of strategy works or is important, don't try to compete with ING Direct. It has returned roughly $4 billion in higher interest rates to its customers while sending about $1.5 billion in operating profit to its parent in Amsterdam over its first seven years of operation.

All this suggests a number of important questions of the kind Kuhlmann had to address.

- Who are your targeted customers (providing market focus), and how does their psychographic profile describe how they think, act, and live?

- What problems are these customers seeking to solve—and which outcomes will they value from your organization?

- What kind of people will you employ, and what value will you offer them?

- Whom don't you wish to hire or serve? What are you doing to screen job candidates and avoid nontarget clients?

- What results do you seek to achieve for targeted customers?

- What package of products and services will be required to deliver them?

- What combination of policies, practices, organization, people, and incentives will be required to achieve operating focus and leverage results and the quality of a customer's experience over costs?

- What kinds of excellence in support systems—information systems, facilities, networks—will this require?

These questions are intended to foster focus, both in the target market and in operations. They represent the basic building blocks of ownership. How would you answer them for your organization?

In our experience, organizations that achieve market focus, such as Whole Foods Markets, can perform very well. Organizations that achieve operating focus, such as United Parcel Service, can expect good performance as well. But organizations that achieve both market and operating focus, such as Vanguard Financial Services and Southwest Airlines—and yes, ING Direct—have changed the face of the industries in which they operate.

The questions help define strategy in terms of value for customers—a combination of results and the quality of the processes that deliver the overall customer experience. And they encourage a search for an effective operating strategy that delivers results in productive, cost-effective ways. Let's start with customers.

TARGETING CUSTOMERS: WHERE'S THE PAIN?

The development of a strategic value vision begins with efforts to identify shifts in the nature of the pain that customers are suffering. Consider, for example, the change that has helped save Rolls-Royce's business.[2] The company used to sell aircraft engines. But it discovered that customers weren't looking only for the best designs. They also wanted to be able to count on the engines to perform. In other words, the product they desired was not engines, but reliable power.

In response, Rolls-Royce launched TotalCare, a program in which airlines pay the company a fee for every hour the engine is in flight. In return, Rolls-Royce assumes responsibility for parts and maintenance. What this arrangement does, of course, is to create an incentive for Rolls-Royce to make sure the engines are operating. As a result, the company's technical force was, as of 2005, remotely monitoring the performance of three thousand of the company's engines for fifty-five airline customers, anticipating maintenance needs and ensuring maximum uptime. In a sense, uptime has come to define the business—and the strategic value vision—at Rolls-Royce, especially because it provides much higher margins than those realized in merely selling the engines, often at highly competitive prices. By launching TotalCare—by moving from a focus on products to a focus on value for customers—Rolls-Royce has aligned its own success with its customers' interests.

Organizations seeking to deliver value continually search out customers' pain to help them correct problems or anticipate needs. IKEA is a good example.[3] Those who don't know the company well assume that it's a manufacturer and retailer of home furnishings—that is, products. Those who frequent the company's stores know that IKEA really provides a socially acceptable way of life for new entrants to the middle class, people who recognize value but are unsure of their taste preferences or of what goes with what. In addition, IKEA offers good design at affordable prices, reinforced by the company's bargaining power, its design capabilities, and its low-cost way of doing business. Customers contribute to low costs by hauling home boxed furniture and assembling it themselves.

In short, IKEA offers a much-needed pain reliever for its targeted customers. But sometimes the company misses its mark. This was the case with Hispanic customers in California. To customize value for its customers, IKEA leveraged its most effective diagnostic tool: visits to the homes of its Hispanic employees and customers. As a result, the company found that its line of products contained items that were not sufficiently colorful, sofas and dining room tables that weren't large enough to accommodate larger Hispanic families, and insufficient numbers and varieties of such things as picture frames. After the company redesigned certain items and remerchandized the stores serving this target market, sales began to increase.

Beyond Demographics: Concentrate on Customer Psychographics and Circumstances

Many organizations define their target customers in terms of demographics: large, small, highly educated, middle-aged, and so on. The data often is easy to acquire, but it is rarely of great value. It is a bit like looking for a lost key at night under a lamppost because the light is better there. The data does at least help scope out the overall size of an opportunity, but only with some additional work to identify customer psychographics.

Psychographics is the study of how customers think, react, behave, and live and therefore the kinds of value they might seek. It takes effort to ferret out this kind of information, often by observation of samples of customers. For example, in developing its personal financial software products, Intuit engages staff in a process called Follow Me Home.[4] Buyers of Intuit products are asked whether they will allow Intuit employees to observe them as they unwrap and install their software and begin to use it. At other times, customers come to the company's headquarters to test new products under the watchful eyes of Intuit's software engineers. They offer a stream-of-consciousness commentary about what they like, what they would like to see in the product, and what they find difficult to use. They are asked how they would use the software and at what times (for purposes of determining service levels)—in short, how they would use Intuit's products to solve problems in their lives.

Find Out Why Customers "Hire" Products or Services

Clayton Christensen and his colleagues have concluded that "customers 'hire' products to do specific 'jobs.'"[5] If this is true, we need to rethink the process of targeting customers. It means that customers with different demographic and psychographic profiles may be buying products or services to relieve more than one kind of pain. Christensen suggests "segmenting markets according to the jobs that customers are trying to get done . . . Companies that target their products at the *circumstances* in which customers find themselves, rather than at the *customers* themselves, are those that can launch predictably successful products."[6]

Even a single customer may have different needs in different circumstances. For example, a man who stops at a fast-food spot on his way to work has a different objective—and seeks a different customer outcome—compared with the same man stopping at the same restaurant with his daughter on a Sunday afternoon.

When Intuit initiated its Follow Me Home program, it learned more about the jobs customers were hiring its products to accomplish. IKEA gleaned similar knowledge from its Hispanic customers and learned to deliver desirable results for a large and growing market.

REDEFINING THE BUSINESS: FROM PRODUCTS AND SERVICES TO VALUE FOR CUSTOMERS

Customers don't buy products or services; they buy value, which comes from a combination of results and the quality of the overall experience in relation to the costs of obtaining them. So doesn't it follow that the purpose of the organization, the business, should be defined in these terms?

This is not a new idea. Nearly fifty years ago, in one of the most widely read business articles of all time, Ted Levitt analyzed the reasons that several declining industries had reached a nadir in their development in the early 1960s. As he put it, "Had Hollywood been customer-oriented (providing entertainment), rather than product-oriented (making movies), would it have gone through the fiscal purgatory that it did?"[7]

Similarly, he concluded that a major reason railroads were in decline at that time was that they viewed themselves as being in the railroad business (product-oriented) as opposed to the transportation business. As a result, railroads were being eclipsed in hauling freight by truckers, water carriers, pipelines, and even high-voltage wires. Shippers had no particular devotion to rail transport. Their pain was felt in getting goods from one place to another by the most reliable and lowest-cost method. In most cases, that was not rail, at least not then. Now, of course, railroads are thriving on the notion that they offer a solution to environmental concerns, a "green" form of transportation. They feature it in their advertising. New pains offer the opportunity of providing new pain relievers.

Years ago, Peter Drucker provided sage advice about defining a business when he suggested that it involved asking three questions: who's my customer? What does my customer want? How do I provide it?[8]

Value-Driven Organizations Innovate and Grow

Organizations that define their mission as making products or delivering services restrict their ability to adapt to changing markets and growth opportunities. In contrast, a focus on delivering value for customers generates opportunities for growth and innovation. Often this takes the form of related diversification. IBM and Best Buy offer prime examples.

IBM. Most often, organizations move from a product-based core to one including service offerings.[9] IBM has been a leader of this trend. It built a huge business around its innovations in computing, particularly by means of the large central processing units found in nearly every large, successful company in the twentieth century. It sold products. In all fairness, it was forced to do so by a 1956 federal decree that required that it divest its service organization from the rest of the company. After that, IBM made only limited forays back into the service business—until the face of computing changed from big box mainframe computers to smaller, distributed, linked units having much greater total capacity. IBM had to rethink its vision for the twenty-first century. It had to think in terms of customer pain. And it has done so with a vengeance.

Sam Palmisano, IBM's CEO, has led a series of forays into pain relief that have resulted in a rethinking of the company's strategic value vision. Early on, it led to IBM's "service on demand" concept, which allowed customers to buy computing capacity from IBM as they needed it, greatly reducing the cost of their information services while expanding the capacity available at periods of peak use. But reportedly, it was at a lunch in 2003 with A. G. Lafley, CEO of Procter & Gamble, that the potential for a new IBM dawned on Palmisano. Lafley shocked Palmisano by estimating that P&G could, if it desired, operate its business with one-fourth of its existing employees by outsourcing various tasks to other organizations. In Palmisano's words, "We saw it as an industry shift."[10] Industry shifts spell pain, and IBM responded with relief. Its business is no longer primarily about products. In fact, it has sold its personal computer business to focus on *transformation*: helping customers run their organizations in totally different ways.

To deliver transformation, IBM set out to remake itself. Among other things, it created the Business Consulting Services group as part of a $46 billion Global Services business. The group is tasked with delivering results to IBM's clients. A part of this process involves helping clients rethink their businesses in terms of pain. Then IBM consultants provide the relief. Its consultants constantly ask clients, "What are you?" Whatever their clients decide (in the case of Virgin Stores, for example, whether it is a line of music stores or lifestyle stores), IBM offers to help them achieve the results they desire. It is little surprise, then, that in early 2004 IBM signed an agreement with Procter & Gamble to run some of P&G's human resource activities in a ten-year, $400 million deal.

IBM's primary competitors are no longer companies that regard themselves as computer manufacturers. Instead, they are consultants (such as EDS and Accenture) as well as the service divisions of companies like Hewlett-Packard and Dell.

Best Buy. Consumer electronics are notoriously low-margin products. Only those retailers that can achieve huge volumes have a chance of success. Let's face it: selling consumer electronics, which at times approach commodity status, is not a very inspiring activity. Further, many of the products create as much pain as they relieve. For example, how many of us know how to make full use of the electronics we buy? Most products have been overdesigned for our needs. Each new feature creates new confusion in the mind of the typical consumer.

Recognizing this, the management of the largest retailer of consumer electronics, Best Buy, bought a company called Geek Squad. Now, the company's Geek Squad technicians stand ready to provide instruction as well as repair services for confused, harassed electronics users.

Geek Squad is a solid source of profit for Best Buy. But it has proven to be much more—a source of new ideas for products and services designed to serve carefully defined customer segments. Geek Squad members detect needs for new products that customers may not even realize. In several cases, this has led to designs that Best Buy takes to suppliers for manufacture. For example, members of one Geek Squad, based on their experiences in the field, developed a new design for an external disk drive for PCs. Only four months later, the company launched the product as part of an expanding line of proprietary products carrying the Best Buy brand.

Geek Squad members also assess the possible demand for new products that haven't yet reached the market. One such effort involved a need on the part of some customers to transfer TV programs from their sets to their PCs. Best Buy reviewed the product development activities of several manufacturers before launching an effort to help bring Slingbox, a product developed by Sling Media, Inc., to market. This process also gave Best Buy an early lead over its competitors in marketing what became a successful product. As Best Buy EVP Ron Boire puts it, "We empower our people to listen and serve, and, at the same time, we go upstream to find out what the suppliers are doing. It's about speed to market. We know what the customers are looking for, and we have a time advantage in getting it to them."[11]

Value-Driven Organizations Are Great Places to Work

Value-driven strategies inspire employees and their managers. It's easy to explain strategic visions based on value, enabling prospective employees to either accept or reject the vision. This helps ensure that you hire only those who subscribe to and can develop a passion for the mission and vision.

Prospective ING Direct employees know whether or not they are orange after only a few minutes spent with company managers; more important, those doing the interviewing know just as quickly.

Even the most mundane jobs provide more satisfaction in firms with value-based strategies. At Best Buy, for example, employees faced with customer complaints are not powerless. Instead of shrugging their shoulders, they have a Geek Squad solution to recommend. Equally important, they know they are collecting ideas for new ways of delivering value for customers.

ALIGNING OPERATING STRATEGY AND SYSTEMS TO DELIVER VALUE

We've spent a great deal of time with outstanding practitioners of owner-ship strategies. Their stories are as diverse as their personalities, capabilities, and strategic value visions. But they all share one thing: they didn't get the operating strategy and support systems right the first time, or for all time. Outstanding operating strategies that provide operational focus to deliver value in extraordinary ways don't just happen overnight. We tend to forget this as we tell and retell legendary success stories, omitting the details of the early days of the enterprise.

For example, in 2006 ING Direct began to encounter competition from large, full-service banks that, until then, had played an important (albeit perhaps unwitting) part in the company's operating strategy. In its early days ING Direct relied heavily on its customers' willingness to maintain their existing checking accounts at the time they switched their savings to ING. In that way, customers retained the convenience of bank checking while earning high interest on their ING savings, transferring money to and from their savings accounts (at no fee) to ensure they had sufficient funds in their checking accounts. Some ING Direct savers were found to be transferring funds daily to provide just the amount of money they planned to spend each day from their checking accounts. This practice enabled ING Direct to shift high-cost services to its full-service banking "partners."

However, a few unwilling partners finally reacted by increasing the value of their offerings to discourage their savers from leaving. Among other things, competitors began offering modest interest on checking account balances. ING Direct's management countered by creating a service known as "Electric Orange," a payment account service activated by customers at very low cost. To encourage them to do so, the company, adhering to its strategic value vision, began paying interest on such accounts roughly comparable to the interest paid on its savings accounts—that is, several times the rate offered by full-service banks. In addition, the company added simple investment service options, such as mutual funds and automatic stock purchase plans, to its line of certificates of deposit, all requiring little sales effort to reach online customers interested in investing some of their savings with ING Direct.

The company's strategic value vision hasn't changed. Everything it offers must be easy for the customer to understand and easy to sell and service. In fact, its value vision has guided continuous improvements in its operating strategy to support its strong growth in both assets and profitability.

AVOIDING COMMON PITFALLS: WHAT CAN GO WRONG

Value-driven strategies lead naturally to a proliferation of products and services intended to solve customer problems. This approach may contain the seeds of competitive disadvantage if not carefully monitored to prevent loss of focus.

The greater your range of products and services, the greater your tendency to cost problem-solving packages on a bundled basis, thereby exposing the organization to competition from those that define the problem more narrowly, essentially picking off portions of solutions at lower cost. This helps explain why ING Direct was able to fashion a successful business by delivering an outstanding package only for savers while full-service banks increasingly expanded products and services to provide a complete financial management capability. It may also help explain why cross-selling of financial products and services has been difficult. Individuals don't seek to solve their overall financial management needs at one time, or even by dealing with only one institution.

It is also why full-service, high-cost organizations find it difficult to offer limited products or services at lower cost. For example, full-service airlines have been notoriously unsuccessful in launching low-cost, limited-service brands. What usually happens when they try to do so? Among other things, they cannot shield the new low-cost start-ups from the established organization. As a result, they succumb to the temptation to force the start-up to hire redundant employees or use redundant aircraft, whether or not they are appropriate to the new strategic value vision. The start-up may be burdened with union rules inherited from its parent that are inappropriate to the task. This practice generally dilutes the focus of the operating strategy, and customer focus may suffer as well.

Loss of operating focus can destroy a company's ability to deliver value for customers and employees alike. Worse, it can cut into profitability, so that even an attractive value vision fails to create a sustainable edge. That's our next concern. To address it, we turn to a set of concepts that helps explain how leading organizations leverage value over costs as they build a strong and sustainable ownership quotient.

Leverage Value over Cost

Organizations that foster ownership gain an edge on the competition by designing their operating strategies and systems to leverage value over cost. They carefully align all the elements of the strategic value vision to create a unified, self-reinforcing enterprise focused on ownership—and in the process they achieve enviable margins. They pay particular attention to what we call *deep indicators*, or key value levers that most influence future performance.

PRAIRIESTONE PHARMACY: GAINING A COMPETITIVE EDGE

Consider, for example, how John Brady, Lew Zeidner, and Marvin Richardson, the founders of PrairieStone Pharmacy, thought about gaining a sustainable edge in delivering value for customers and employees.

Despite the relatively high earnings opportunities in the field, there is a puzzling shortage of pharmacists in the United States. The job often consists largely of counting out pills ("counting by fives," in the trade jargon) and then dispensing them to customers the pharmacists don't know, customers who may be irritated by having to stand in line or return later to get their prescriptions. The pharmacist has little or no chance to interact with customers or to offer meaningful advice, and the resulting lack of information may help explain why two-thirds of us who need the medications either don't take them or take them incorrectly.[1] In short, often we have bored people serving largely unknown, uninformed, and perhaps irritated and anxious customers.

PrairieStone Pharmacy, a chain of micro-pharmacies that both literally and figuratively delivers pain relief on the premises of several U.S. supermarket chains, is trying to change this. Its comprehensive, self-reinforcing operating strategy and support systems leverage multiple sources of value for employees as well as customers, at costs lower than those of its more conventional competitors.

PrairieStone's value vision for customers offers convenience, 100 percent accuracy in medications, and a pleasant experience in which pharmacists spend roughly 40 percent more time speaking with customers than in a typical pharmacy. The company describes its idealized target customer, "Heather," as the oldest female in the family, who shops at the supermarket an average of 2.3 times per week. The pain she suffers is concern for the health of her family, including aging parents or other loved ones. She values convenience and the opportunity to consult with an engaging pharmacist. Although she may be less price sensitive than some, when she compares PrairieStone's prices with other pharmacies (something she is rarely motivated to do), she finds that she pays no more than at other pharmacies where she receives much less personal attention. She enjoys the benefits of PrairieStone's efforts and expresses her satisfaction to her friends, encouraging them to patronize her favorite pharmacy. As a result, a significant percentage of PrairieStone's business derives from customer referrals.

PrairieStone Pharmacy has gone to great lengths to make believers and owners of its customers, its pharmacists and technicians, and its distribution partners as well. Among other things, it has literally turned the typical pharmacy on its side, thereby reducing the footprint of its shops to 413 square feet, less than half that of the typical pharmacy.[2] Prairie-Stone has taken advantage of high supermarket ceilings to design a fourteen-foot-high vertical carousel that operates automatically from an order-processing computer into which pharmacists enter prescriptions; pharmacy assistants (technicians) then assemble the orders rapidly without searching shelves. The carousel is large enough to contain more drugs than a typical pharmacy, and that facilitates the filling of multiple prescriptions in one visit.

PrairieStone relies on this high-speed, high-volume automated technology to fill as many as four hundred prescriptions per day in each of its twenty-eight pharmacies. This technology is typically found only in clinical pharmacy settings. It uses bar codes to direct the entire process of counting, labeling, capping, record keeping, and inventory control. It enables the company to cut prescription fill times while increasing interactions between pharmacists and patients. And it offers a special kind of pain relief in the form of DailyMed, a service that presorts multiple prescriptions, over-the-counter medications, and vitamins into single-dose packets for forgetful patients.

This automation gives pharmacists more time to devote to customers, who are invited to sit down while consulting with "their" pharmacist, with whom they may have made an appointment. PrairieStone seeks out experienced as well as graduating pharmacists who want to spend more time with customers. Not all pharmacists want to do that. But having found the ones who do, the company provides them with a superior working environment as well as a job that involves spending less time counting pills and more time counseling customers. Similarly, it hires pharmacy assistants who enjoy working with technology and want to be part of a growing organization, and trains them to operate the computer-driven prescription-filling technology.

Katie Kelly, pharmacy manager for a PrairieStone pharmacy, puts it this way: "I am forming relationships with patients. I know them by their first name. They build a trusting relationship with you. You know what medications they are taking. Having time to talk to patients about their medications is the best thing about working at PrairieStone."[3]

For the Katie Kellys of the pharmacist community, PrairieStone provides value in the form of a competitive compensation package as well as superior working conditions. A PrairieStone pharmacy is, in a sense, a pharmaceutical computer staffed with owners. Its operating strategy is supported by unique facilities and first-rate technology.

Employee loyalty is high at PrairieStone. There is no shortage of talent waiting for jobs there, even though pharmacists are in great demand. Word gets around fast, and it is fueled by referrals from PrairieStone's employees. Turnover is low, ensuring that particularly its older customers—who are issued, on average, thirty-five prescriptions per year—see the same familiar faces next to them, and not behind a counter. This practice again creates an edge for PrairieStone, its employees, and its customers.

PrairieStone pharmacists still need to check the prescriptions before dispensing them. But because the packing system puts all prescriptions in clear bags, it's easy to verify them, and, in the process, the system leverages a valued result for customers (accurately filled prescriptions) over labor costs. The DailyMed prescription packets add further value by ensuring the accurate consumption of prescriptions, another important customer result for doctors and their patients. There is no added cost for this: the operating strategy and systems deliver it automatically as part of PrairieStone's strategic value vision (see figure 3-1). It should be no surprise that PrairieStone fills the same number of prescriptions in less than half the space needed by its competitors, creating another value lever for the company, its customers, and its host stores.

In sum, PrairieStone's strategic value vision fosters ownership among employees and customers alike—but not by sacrificing profit. Far from it. Thanks to the leveraging of space, talent, and time, the cost of the preparation and delivery of prescriptions is actually less than at other pharmacies. And the employee and customer owners help fuel growth and profitability. If you put all these elements together, as PrairieStone has, you will gain a sustainable competitive edge.

FIGURE 3-1

PrairieStone Pharmacy's strategic value vision

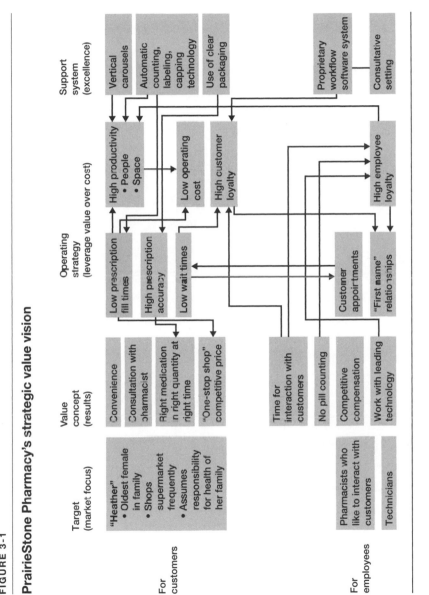

CREATING VALUE COST-EFFECTIVELY: WHY LEVERAGE IS CRUCIAL

Leveraging value over cost is at the heart of an operating strategy for any organization. PrairieStone's founders understand that value for customers means more than just the accurate filling of prescriptions; it also has to do with *process quality*—or how the results are delivered—something that enhances the customer's overall experience.

They also understand that costs to the customer may be more than the cost of the prescription, particularly if the pharmacy is not located conveniently, is not open when prescriptions are needed, or cannot fill prescriptions quickly to minimize waiting time. These inconveniences represent access costs for the customer. In short, PrairieStone understands the basic elements of the customer value equation, which codifies the central concept of customer value articulated in chapter 2.

Define Your Customer Value Equation

We use the following set of relationships to represent value for customers:

$$\text{Value for Customers} = \frac{\text{Results + Quality of the Experience}}{\text{Total Cost (Price + Access Costs)}}$$

We distilled this equation based on analysis of extensive marketing research data from the companies we have observed and worked with over several decades. In many cases, customers' reactions reflect the quality of the experience more heavily than results. Think of your own experiences. At a minimum, you probably require that anything you purchase will deliver the results you expect. Inadequate results combined with an outstanding overall experience (including service recovery, free repair, and so on) might still preserve your loyalty to a product or a service. But expected results combined with a poor overall experience (an abusive or dismissive salesperson, delayed shipment, and so on) can often produce the opposite effect.

Viewed from inside the company, the quality of experience for customers is a function of process quality. If both results and process quality are excellent, the customers are more likely to enjoy positive and memorable experiences. And if the company emphasizes the value levers that matter most, it is more likely to enhance its ownership quotient. Let's examine how this plays out at PrairieStone Pharmacy.

Your pharmacist at PrairieStone is available by appointment. When you arrive, she is not rushed; she invites you to sit down to discuss your ailment and gives you advice about how to take a medicine to minimize side effects. While this is going on, your prescription is being filled accurately, in handy daily dosages if you prefer. Not only is the quality of the process high, but also it achieves the results you seek as part of an agreeable overall experience.

The automated picking system speeds the preparation of prescriptions, so you can pick up your order in a single visit—and do some grocery shopping, too—thereby reducing access costs in the denominator of the customer value equation. And PrairieStone delivers all this value at prices no higher than you would pay elsewhere.

So the customer value equation for PrairieStone Pharmacies looks like this:

$$\text{Customer Value} = \frac{[\text{Results (accurately filled prescriptions, daily doses)}] + [\text{Quality of Experience (little or no waiting, consultation with pharmacists)}]}{[\text{Price (lowest in the area, consultation with pharmacists to reduce total cost)}] + [\text{Access Costs (easy access inside supermarkets, no second visits to pick up prescriptions)}]}$$

All the elements in PrairieStone's customer value equation matter, and they are carefully coordinated to deliver valued results, high process quality, and low access costs, with relatively high margins due to the company's own low costs. But the availability of pharmacists for customer counseling appears to have the greatest influence in increasing customer loyalty and referrals. Time spent in consultations, then, may be one of PrairieStone's key value levers for customer ownership. It may be a deep indicator that predicts a sense of ownership in customers, and therefore future performance. As you'll see in chapter 5, the consultation experience is also a key value lever in building employee ownership. The result is a solidly profitable pharmacy with an impressive ownership quotient and a formidable edge over the competition.

Manage the Key Value Levers

Companies often find their key sources of leverage in the deep indicators they track to predict financial and nonfinancial results. Deep indicators are never revenue, cost, profit, or other financial measures; these are lagging indicators or effects. In contrast, deep or leading indicators are the true drivers of success.

Leaders who can engineer employee and customer ownership understand how to leverage the deep indicators across organizational functions such as marketing, operations, information technology, and human resources. They know how to recognize and manage their key value levers, including the following:

- The definition and delivery of the overall experience for customers as well as employees

- The design of mutually reinforcing processes, jobs, and facilities

- The choice of technology to support these operations

- The attributes of prospective employees

- The structure and systems that organize the work

- The nature of performance metrics and incentives

USING KEY VALUE LEVERS TO TRANSFORM NYPD

When Rudolph Giuliani, then mayor of New York, appointed William Bratton police commissioner in 1994, New York was considered one of the most dangerous big cities in the United States.[4] Bratton knew he would have to be innovative in order to make progress in reducing crime, because Giuliani had promised no budget increases for policing.

At the time, NYPD was at its best in responding to 9-1-1 emergency calls for assistance. As Bratton put it, "We were very good at getting to the scene of a crime 30 minutes after the perpetrators had left."[5] Existing policies rewarded effort, not results. A student of management, Bratton knew that he needed to develop the equivalent of a strategic value vision for the people in the department as well as for the citizens on the street. He focused first on what he saw as deep indicators for reducing crime: citizens' perception of police work, community cooperation, and the ability to anticipate and prevent criminal behavior.

Even though Bratton had only about twenty-four months to achieve the expected results, the changes he and his team implemented transformed New York from a haven for criminals to one of the safest large cities in the United States. In our opinion, he changed the face of policing throughout the world by recognizing the deep indicators and managing the key levers of value for NYPD.

Redefining the Customer–Police Officer Experience

Commissioner Bratton began by insisting that NYPD start thinking of citizens as customers. In the early 1990s, the quality of the NYPD customer experience was mediocre at best. Customers were more likely to be at the wrong end of a summons issued by a police officer than to receive services that they could value. It often took months to solve crimes, with police engaged in time-consuming work in preparing for and testifying at trials rather than solving crimes.

It was hard to find a police officer when one was needed; they were often patrolling in vehicles rather than walking the streets. Or they were working at hours and in places that were convenient for them rather than at times or places where the probability of crime was highest. There was an adversarial relationship between the police and the citizens they were charged to protect. As a result, police received little cooperation from ordinary citizens who may have witnessed crimes.

The employee experience was little better. Police officers had to cope with outmoded equipment, inadequate information, and even protective equipment of dubious safety. They spent a great deal of time filling out reports. These problems, combined with low conviction rates in court, made them reluctant to press charges in cases that should have been pursued more vigorously. Sick-leave rates were high; morale was low. And still, with the pride of being members of perhaps the world's best-known police department—one that inspired a popular television series—police officers didn't want to talk about any of this. It wasn't until the new commissioner brought in an outside psychologist to conduct a "cultural diagnosis" that officers began to talk. And they hated every minute of it.

Redesigning Processes, Jobs, and Facilities

Bratton used the cultural diagnosis to support an extensive reengineering effort and streamline operations at NYPD. This work involved improving processes, reassigning people, and upgrading everything from facilities to the weaponry and protective equipment issued to police officers.

As one example of this extensive process reengineering project, Bratton and his colleagues persuaded the judiciary to permit remote police officer testimony, using two-way television, in many routine cases being heard in court. This practice, combined with improved methods of reporting crimes and filing evidence, reduced the time officers spent in court-required administrative tasks by more than 80 percent. It eliminated many tasks the officers despised and freed their time for more meaningful jobs.

One of the more significant personnel moves was to reassign police officers from administrative work at headquarters and precinct stations to positions closer to citizens and the locus of crime, a move applauded by officers on the street. More officers were assigned to street duty instead of police cruisers. At first most of the officers opposed this move. But as some of them acquainted themselves with neighborhoods and their institutions, they gained skills in anticipating problems that might lead to crimes and following up with successful investigations when crimes actually occurred. Those who succeeded found value in their new capabilities, and others who were not cut out for this kind of work were reassigned to other jobs.

Choosing the Right Technology

In a discussion of policing technology, most people focus on weaponry or squad car accessories. But the most important piece of technology introduced at NYPD was an information system called CompStat, which assembles and reports information about major elements of crime, including such things as the location of people with previous criminal records, places where drugs are reported to be bought and sold, and gun ownership. When compared with continual updates of statistics con cerning crimes, CompStat enabled commanders of New York's seventy-six precincts to begin mapping strategies for reducing major crimes. Just as important, CompStat helped clarify the discussions at the precinct commanders' weekly Monday morning meetings, enabling them to present and report on their strategies and receive meaningful feedback from other commanders. In the process it raised the visibility of precinct police leadership and sharpened everyone's effort.

Selecting the Right People

To succeed in reducing crime in a department previously focused on effort, Commissioner Bratton first had to make sure his people believed that leadership could have an impact on crime reduction. There were many naysayers among sociologists, economists, and criminologists, who believed that crime rates were rooted in poverty, unemployment, and education and not in police work. Further, precinct commanders had to believe in a different theory of fighting crime, one that advocated the arrest of individuals for petty crimes on the belief that petty criminals also carried the guns and other weapons that would someday contribute to major crimes. Implementing that theory would require more effort.

In fact, two-thirds of Bratton's precinct commanders were not willing to subscribe to the notion that crime could be managed. Because he couldn't fire them, Bratton had to find other jobs for them. He also changed the recruiting process to winnow out candidates whose main interest in becoming a police officer was the chance to carry a gun or to exercise power over others.

Changing Structure and Systems

A hierarchy of civilian and police personnel had taken hold at NYPD headquarters over the years. As a result, commanders had limited responsibility for what went on in their respective precincts. But if customized responses to the problems of a particular neighborhood were to be devised, these were the very people who would have to lead such an effort. So Bratton gave precinct commanders full responsibility and authority for what happened in their precincts, eliminated several layers of management, and created a post in his office to which all precinct commanders reported directly.

Refining Performance Metrics and Incentives

What gets measured gets done, according to the adage. So Bratton changed performance metrics to track the things that matter most in combating crime. Instead of the number of 9-1-1 calls answered or the number of summonses issued, all the important measures became associated with results such as community involvement, response time, and other deep indicators for reducing major crimes.

But what does one do when the police union and civil service rules make it nearly impossible to pay monetary incentives for good performance in a police department? And when the one possible monetary incentive—pay for overtime—was being targeted for drastic cutting to meet budgetary goals? One improvises. At NYPD, Bratton and his team found ways to recognize everything from heroic acts to good, basic police work. These incentives included rewarding top performers with the best work schedules and even giving them time off with pay.

BUILDING ON DEEP INDICATORS AT VICTORIA'S SECRET

Nowhere are the key value levers managed more consciously and effectively than at Victoria's Secret (VS), a chain of approximately one thousand lingerie stores that master merchant Leslie Wexner has built from his purchase of six somewhat rundown San Francisco area stores operating under that name in 1982.[6] From that modest beginning, the brand has sought to become synonymous with "sexy," in the process capturing nearly 26 percent of all bra sales and a large share of all the lingerie sold in the United States. Its stores sell as much as $3,000 in merchandise per square foot annually—ten times that of some of its competitors—while providing a distinctive shopping experience for youthful customers of all ages and margins greater than 40 percent for shareholders of its parent, Limited Brands.

The strategic value vision at Victoria's Secret requires a constant flow of new designs that offer improved fit, comfort, materials, and style at affordable prices. Beyond that, it requires store designs that create a kind of refuge where women can choose lingerie while enjoying appropriate background music and images of VS supermodels wearing the products.

Limited Brands and Victoria's Secret have identified the deep indicators of value and profitability in their business model and have learned to manage them almost as a science. For example, real estate costs are very high at the preferred locations for Victoria's Secret stores. So one deep indicator that management uses to leverage value is *store productivity* (sales per square foot). Customer traffic and conversion rates, along with the average size of the sales transaction, are key determinants of sales per square foot. These, combined with a measure of the percentage of goods sold at the initial markup (IMU), in turn help predict profitability.

Conversion rates (the proportion of shoppers entering a store who actually make a purchase) are especially important: each 1 percent increase in the conversion rate is worth $35 million in sales, and more than $15 million in operating profit, to the Victoria's Secret brand. That makes conversion rates a powerful deep indicator to be managed.

Traffic is a function of the effectiveness of promotional activity, store location, and the attractiveness of the store. Conversion rates and average size of sales transactions, on the other hand, are a function of the availability of desirable merchandise along with salespeople who are capable of closing sales. That's why VS's real-time labor management tools, which enable employees to be transferred in and out of sales roles as needed, are critical. And it explains why the company places a great deal of emphasis on the selection and training of new associates, whether or not they have previous work experience.

Volume is one thing; profit is another. That's why the proportion of total sales at *initial markup* is another critical deep indicator. It requires that the right merchandise be on hand at the right time, supplemented by Victoria's Secret merchandise managers, who understand how and when to take markdowns for maximum profit.

In retailing, success breeds success. So Victoria's Secret can wield considerable leverage in obtaining the best retail sites (primarily in malls) for its kind of business. This practice in itself fosters sales by positioning the stores in the natural shopping paths of potential customers.

Let's explore how the operating strategy and support systems use these deep indicators to leverage value at Victoria's Secret, as outlined in figure 3-2. As you will see, the ultimate measure of alignment among the elements of an operating strategy is the degree to which one element makes another possible.

Creating the Experience

Picture the Victoria's Secret flagship store in Herald Square in New York City—at thirty thousand square feet, the largest and most costly lingerie store location in the world. On a busy day, more than two hundred associates realize several hundred thousand dollars' worth of sales there. The inside of the store is a riot of color and music in the beauty and lingerie sections. It offers a number of internally developed brands as well as those of recently added partner Intimissimi, an Italian producer and

FIGURE 3-2

Operating strategy and support systems at Victoria's Secret

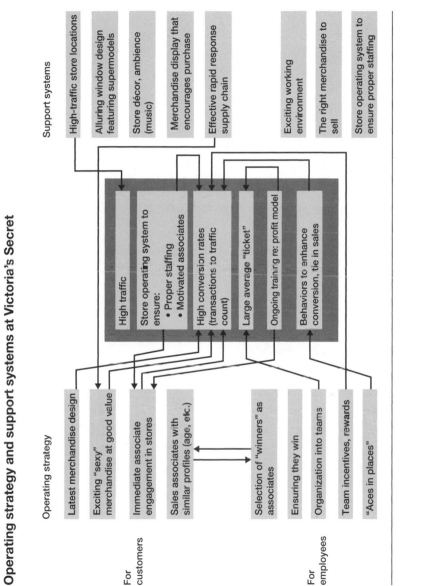

European retailer of similarly priced lingerie. The effect is one of plenty, with a wide selection.

The store is staffed with young associates hired for their friendly attitudes. They are often the same age as target customers, adding to the experience for customers as well as associates. As many as one in three visitors makes a purchase (a conversion rate of 33 percent). This result creates the sense among associates that they are achieving results for customers, making the work experience even more positive for them.

VS stores are designed to promote expectations of a pleasurable shopping experience, drawing high traffic to strategically located premises. Thus, VS can operate with limited traditional advertising and generally low promotional costs. The company's signal promotional event—the annual fashion show—is broadcast on national television, attracting a huge audience and reinforcing the Victoria's Secret brand image at a modest cost. Store designs encourage browsing and self-service (for example, large drawers containing panties are posted with signs that invite shoppers to open and go through them); ample numbers of checkout stations have simple touch screen registers that minimize the need for training and can be placed in service quickly to minimize customer waiting time.

Designing Mutually Reinforcing Processes, Jobs, and Facilities

No single idea or operations initiative explains the success of truly outstanding value-producing organizations. Instead, it is the internal consistency of the ideas, policies, practices, controls, and organization, backed up by excellent support systems working in a mutually reinforcing way to leverage value over cost. Each element of the operating strategy is linked to others. The more linkages and the better the internal coordination, the greater the self-reinforcement among components of the strategy, and the stronger a sustainable edge it creates for the organization.

Behind the Victoria's Secret brand and experience are carefully engineered processes, jobs, and facilities. Consider, for example, a bra. It is a highly engineered item of apparel. As a result, the design stage for a new bra style can be prolonged. Getting the new style to market may take even longer. To maintain its dominance in the category, VS controls the design and manufacturing processes for nearly all of the lingerie sold in its stores. As a result, the company has created a "rapid response" supply chain to introduce a steady stream of new styles, thus contributing to in-store excitement.

The name of the game at Victoria's Secret is converting store traffic to sales having as large an average ticket as possible. To make this happen, VS needs great merchants to pick the best products, great designers to create them, and a supply chain that gets them to the right stores at the right times and in the right amounts. At all times, stores need to have ample supplies of basic items that customers buy most. (Management's euphemism for this is the classic "34B" bra. If you run out of that item, no amount of value or experience will trigger a sale.)

The company screens potential associates carefully, selects those with the strongest ability to relate to customers, supports them with state of-the-art point-of-sale technology, and rewards them when they exceed sales goals.

Victoria's Secret designs its jobs and support systems to foster winners. Young women, many of them in their first jobs, comprise the vast majority of frontline associates. Advanced information systems guide staff-scheduling plans to accommodate traffic patterns and peaks. On a busy day in a large store, for example, more than one hundred associates may be working at one time. An individual may perform more than one job during a given shift, so all associates receive training in all tasks in the store. When traffic builds, those in the stockroom unpacking merchandise may be shifted to the sales floor for a period of time. Jobs are designed to be done under the pressure of large numbers of customers. For example, the cash wrap routine for customers making purchases has been designed to minimize time and effort on the part of associates and to increase checkout convenience for customers, as described in greater detail in "Line-Busting Technology at Victoria's Secret."

Line-Busting Technology at Victoria's Secret

At the store level, the *Victoria's Secret* flagship in New York's Herald Square has emerged as "a real technology incubator, as well as a significant stores system process incubator," Jon J. Ricker, president and chief information officer, The Limited Technology Services, said. "It's a completely wireless store." He explained that the POS operates on a wireless network, with registers that transmit sales data every night back to the home office, and mobile POS configured to process credit-card transactions, gift-card transactions, open new credit accounts, or preprocess transactions so there's less time taken at the wrap desk, where lines can be long. They work on the persistent network connection online, instead of dialing into a credit authorization provider.

The store for the past three months has been testing this "line-busting" technology. To preprocess a transaction, an associate scans items using a mobile point of sale, from Symbol Technologies, also known as an "m-pos." What's viewed on the m-pos screen is the same as on a register screen.

On crowded days, such as the Victoria's Secret semi-annual sale period, the line-buster is stationed at a table not far from the wrap desk. After the items are scanned, the customer receives a receipt that isn't itemized. The line-buster can also remove the security tag, and customers are carefully watched to see that they don't head straight for the door, instead of to the checkout line.

Meanwhile, the information gets automatically uploaded at the register so by the time the customer gets there, all the associate behind the counter needs to do is scan a bar code on the receipt, and the customer then gets an itemized receipt. The procedure cuts down the time at the wrap desk by two to three minutes or by 30 percent on average per transaction, making for faster-moving lines. The line-buster technology, while capable of completing transactions, is primarily being used for preprocessing transactions.[a]

a. David Moin, "The Limited Way," *Women's Wear Daily*, January 9, 2004.

Harnessing Technology to Promote Deep Indicators

Technology plays an important part in creating and maintaining the Victoria's Secret experience. Sophisticated computer-aided design and manufacturing systems transmit designs and track manufacturing processes for lingerie produced mainly in Southeast Asia. The finished merchandise is flown to Columbus, Ohio, and then flows to stores according to pull systems, which track customer sales (rather than push systems, which track production output).

But again, it's in the stores where technology comes to the fore. A labor-scheduling routine, ACES, enables managers to schedule as many as two hundred associates per store in a matter of minutes per week rather than the day and a half per week that was required to do it manually. Further, the technology feeds sales information into the store's point-of-sale machines and compares it with targets for time periods as short as two hours; it displays green, yellow, and red signals to indicate, respectively, whether the associate team working the sales floor is on track to meet its two-hour sales goal, is falling behind, or is likely to miss the target.

Store traffic is counted electronically and compared with transactions to report conversion rates on a real-time basis. A manager noticing low conversion rates on her point-of-sale device can move additional associates from the back room to the sales floor to take advantage of store traffic and increase conversion rates. In a store setting that resembles a boudoir, little is left to chance.

Choosing the Right Employee Attributes

Victoria's Secret hires for attitude: it seeks associates with engaging personalities who can interact with customers and provide at least a modicum of advice and assistance when required. The other necessary skills can be taught quickly on the job, and support systems can ensure success for someone who has the desired attitude. But an associate also must be able to work well in cooperation with other members of a sales team.

The job requires a person who can adapt quickly to one or more task assignments on a single work shift, someone who finds this range of tasks part of the excitement of working at Victoria's Secret.

Finding the Right Structure and Support Systems

Les Wexner has always believed in leveraging the benefits of decentralization and in placing profit responsibility nearest the customer. As a result, senior managers with operating profit responsibility run Victoria's Secret and Limited Brands' other megabrands, including Bath & Body Works and Henri Bendel. These managers are directly responsible for merchant activities such as the selection of styles and lines of products. They must also marshal the necessary support from centrally provided systems that specialize in design, supply chain, information technology, and even store operations. The organization reflects the difficulty of finding brand leaders who have both merchant and operating knowledge, interests, and skills.

Aligning Performance Metrics and Incentives with Deep Indicators

Performance metrics and incentives are most effective when they reflect the deep indicators that drive the business and create the most leverage. They also reflect the things that associates at each level of the organization value.

At the store level, for example, Victoria's Secret offers wages that are, on average, a bit higher than the market. Benefits include associate discounts on merchandise. The company also endeavors to make the working environment as exciting for associates as for customers. It pays added incentives when sales teams accomplish their one-, two-, or four-hour sales goals. But these financial incentives may not be as important as the impromptu ways in which store managers create excitement for associates, ranging from in-store training to contests based on measures other than sales. Because associates work in teams for a given shift, the incentives typically are team based.

Store managers can create short-term contests based on deep indicators such as traffic and conversion rates or the average size of a sales transaction. For store managers, base compensation may be slightly lower than market wages, but substantial opportunity exists to realize bonuses based on store performance.

THE BOTTOM LINE: DIVIDING A LARGER PIE

The difference between value to the customer (results plus the quality of the experience) and the cost incurred in creating the value determines the size of the pie to be split between employees' incentive payments, customers, and investors. The difference between value and what the customer pays in money and time is a way of thinking about that share of the pie that goes to the customer. It may vary from one customer to the next.

The difference between price and cost, which roughly equates to operating profit, is often greatest when the customer is more interested in the numerator (results + quality of the experience) than the denominator (price + access costs) of the customer value equation. When that happens, customers become less price sensitive and more willing to pay a premium for the products or services they desire. This willingness results in a larger share of the pie for employee incentives, reinvestment in the business, and returns to investors.

The reason that margins are high at Victoria's Secret is that the company has built a competitive edge. A VS shopper doesn't come away with products and services alone. She gets a positive shopping experience for just the right lingerie—and, more important, lingerie that fits and is flattering to her ego—and these constitute a self-reinforcing set of results that she considers well worth the price.

At this point, you may be saying that what works at PrairieStone, NYPD, and Victoria's Secret won't work with your kind of business. Darlene Elder, managing director of Bear and Human Resources for

Build-A-Bear Workshop®, the retailer of stuffed animals and interactive animal-making experiences, has a word of advice in this regard:

> Because we deliver an experience—and do it well enough that it looks easy, which it is not—other companies have questioned how they can deliver the same "wow" experience for their clients in industries that may not include a "bear-hug test" as part of their day-to-day operations. There are many great companies out there that have figured out how to deliver a positive experience for their customer and their associates. It's about the special things that you do as a company that make you stand out. We are committed to redefining retail by providing fun and having fun for customers and for associates. But companies in every industry can make a difference in their own way.[7]

For any kind of business, leveraging value over cost provides the opportunity to realize higher margins than competitors, margins that can support added investment in customer and employee ownership. We turn next to ways of putting customers to work that not only leverage long-term value over cost but also increase the ownership quotient in the process.

4

Put Customers to Work

Charlene Otto, global external relations officer at Procter & Gamble, has commented, "Now more than ever, consumers own our brands. Consumers own our messages. Consumers own the conversation about how, where and if they invite our brands into their lives."[1] Her point was that marketers have diminishing control over the messages they communicate.

That may be bad news for some. The good news is that many customers will put themselves to work for their favorite brands. Some even are enthusiastic about helping create the specific outcomes they desire. And with that chance to control some aspects of their purchase comes an expanded sense of ownership.

Diane Hessan, president and CEO of Communispace Corp., which creates private online customer communities specifically designed to create ongoing dialogue between companies and their customers, has a very specific point of view on the subject. She knows from experience that "companies have to earn this kind of customer ownership." They must listen intensely and react appropriately. And when they do, Hessan says "it blows customers away."[2]

John Fleming and Jim Asplund have created a short set of questions to identify customers who are fully engaged, engaged, or actively disengaged

Customer Owners at Work at Karmaloop

Each week, Greg Selkoe, founder of streetwear retailer Karmaloop, and a handful of his employees gather in his office overlooking Boston Common to review new designs. The group votes on which, if any, of the T-shirts, jackets, and other clothing should be added to the line Karmaloop sells in its Newbury Street store and online. That may sound a lot like what goes on at most retailers, but what Karmaloop is doing is very different, and not just because the company's thirty-two-year-old chief executive at times interrupts discussion to blast a tune through the camouflage-covered speakers attached to his PC. What's worth noting is that the designs are submitted by customers. Since October [2006], 37 designs, out of about 1,000 that have been submitted, have been added to the 33-employee, $4 million company's offerings. Selling clothing dreamt up by customers is just one facet of a business model that brings customers so far into Karmaloop's DNA that they have become, in effect, extensions of the company's sales, marketing, and product development teams. Karmaloop has an 8,000-strong army of customers who proselytize the brand and get discounts or cash when they, or someone they've referred, make a purchase. Members of this "street team," called reps, also upload images, photos, or artwork to

with a given organization.[3] They ask questions that measure both *attitudinal loyalty* (satisfaction, likelihood of repeat purchase, and likelihood of recommending to a friend or associate) and *emotional attachment* (trust, delivery on expectations, fair treatment, and so on). Not surprisingly, these authors have found that fully engaged customers represent a 23 percent premium over average customers in share of wallet, profitability, revenue, and relationship growth. Actively disengaged customers, on the other hand, represent a 13 percent discount from the average on these same measures.

Fully engaged customers are potential owners who can help customize the aspects of value that mean the most to them. Most self-selecting customer owners prefer the control that goes with greater input into

Karmaloop's site to make company stickers or banners other reps can download. "The reps are evangelists for our site," says Selkoe. And they're doing their job: Fewer than 1 percent of Karmaloop's customers are reps, but their purchases and those they inspire account for 15 percent of sales.

CEOs have been talking about customer loyalty for years, but entrepreneurs such as Selkoe know that making people truly loyal to your company—to make them really, really like you—takes a lot more than a frequent buyer program. It means nothing less than getting people so jazzed about your brand that they become engaged contributors to your company's sales, marketing, and innovation efforts, and ultimately its success. How does that happen? By knocking down the walls between "you" and "them" and creating a larger, looser community that is inviting to both your customers and your employees.

Selkoe admits that building a community around a brand is a natural fit for his four-year-old company, which courts young, artistic, and Web-savvy customers with the credo that Karmaloop was founded "to battle the evil forces of McFashion." But companies old and young, consumer and business-to-business, can employ similar tactics.[a]

a. Amy Barrett, "True Believers," *BusinessWeek SmallBiz*, Winter 2006, 47–48.

the process. Many gain a great deal of satisfaction from this work, as evidenced in more than one study of customer behavior.

"Customer Owners at Work at Karmaloop" describes how one small company engages its customers to help create value. It's a simple, young organization, but it illustrates the concept well.

ENCOURAGING CUSTOMERS TO HELP CREATE VALUE

To put customers to work effectively, you need to consider several important questions: what kind of work is most appropriate for customers? Why do they choose to work for (or against) a brand? How should you design and manage their jobs? What limits do they place on their participation? What do they expect in return? And what can go wrong with schemes to involve the customer?

Identify the Work That Customers Perform Best

Customers deliver service, improve processes, sell, and even manufacture or assemble products. They are most likely to pitch in when they can participate in shaping one or more elements of the customer value equation we introduced in chapter 3: results, overall experience, price, or access costs. Some do it to save money or time. Others do it to gain control over results and process quality. Still others do it to avoid unwanted personal interactions. And some do it out of desperation. But most often, they involve themselves willingly and with enthusiasm.

Delivering Service. Successful do-it-yourself strategies most often satisfy several motives at once. For example, gasoline service stations usually provide clear price comparisons between full-serve and self-serve pumps so that customers know how much money they save by doing the work themselves. Many customers think they're also saving time, and some prefer to avoid interacting with an attendant in a task they consider a nuisance at best.[4]

Customers may be more effective than professionals in performing services when they or their acquaintances are the immediate beneficiaries, as in nearly all medical and other personal services. For example, research has shown that patients are more expert than health professionals in administering pain control medications. They control pain more effectively with less painkiller, mainly because they have better information about what they need and how often they need it.

Nowhere are customers put to work more effectively than at Shouldice Hospital in Toronto, and the resulting sense of ownership is remarkable.[5] Shouldice's targeted, for-profit strategic value vision employs surgeons who specialize in repairing inguinal hernias, a condition that most often afflicts men. In fact, the surgeons repair more than eight thousand hernias per year—and they engage their patients as partners in the process.

Prospective patients begin by completing a questionnaire that enables the staff to determine whether they actually have a hernia and whether they qualify for immediate surgery or must first lose weight. The most important thing about the questionnaire—and, in some cases, the subsequent dieting—is that it sends the message that Shouldice expects patients to take charge of their own treatment.

The hospital reinforces this notion when patients arrive for surgery. New arrivals learn what to expect by talking to other patients who have just had their operations. In turn, the incoming patients are expected to counsel other newcomers after their own operations. Together, the patients review research that links faster recovery times to a prescribed exercise regimen. They even shave the affected area themselves before the operation. And when the operation, performed with a local anesthetic, is complete, patients are expected to walk from the operating table as a first step in taking charge of what typically is a quick recovery.

When carried out in the company of many others who are undergoing the same treatment in a country club–like setting, this seeming do-it-yourself medicine becomes an unforgettable social experience. Like those who have served in battle together, the patients make quick and deep connections. In fact, many are not ready to leave when their treatment is complete. Many have told staff members that they look forward to the hospital-sponsored annual reunion dinner, the price of admission to which is a quick hernia inspection.

Hernia operations at Shouldice cost less than half those at other North American hospitals. The rate of recurrence is less than one-tenth the average for North American hospitals; in other words, quality is more than ten times the average. Surgeons and the limited number of staff members required in this do-it-yourself process are paid very well. And the clinic still earns a high rate of profit. Is this too good to be true? Not when carefully targeted customers behaving as owners work alongside the hospital staff to achieve world-class results, enhanced process quality, and a valued overall experience.

Improving Products or Services. Referrals, recommendations, and condemnations have become a way of life for an increasing army of Internet users who thrive on networking. Following Amazon.com's pioneering example, many organizations invite their Web site visitors to comment on things they've bought, read, or watched. Angie's List offers a service centered on users' recommendations for plumbers, carpenters, and other service providers they have engaged through the service. Another prime example is Wikipedia, the online encyclopedia where anyone may add information or "correct" (for better or worse) perceived misinformation. Customers participate in this kind of community effort to help improve the quality of the information on the site.

InterContinental Hotel Group (IHG) has gained valuable insights and has adopted many suggestions from its online forum for frequent travelers. Faster and easier to manage than traditional focus groups, the community has improved the company's time to market for new products and services while reducing marketing costs by as much as 90 percent, as described in "InterContinental Hotels Cultivates Customer Web Community to Improve Business."

Producing Personal Value. Increasingly, customers have begun to take charge of transporting and assembling the products they buy, with an enthusiasm some call the "IKEA effect." IKEA customers, subscribing to its "global cult brand" of home furnishings, have for years carted their purchases home and assembled them themselves, thus greatly reducing costs for some of the most vexing steps in selling and distributing home furnishings.[6]

IKEA's stores have large, attractive display spaces so that customers can envision how their purchases might look at home. Just as important, the items on display are designed for easy shipment in a disassembled form. To facilitate the do-it-yourself delivery process, IKEA maintains greater-than-normal inventories, so increased warehouse space is a must. But without clearly presented assembly instructions and the right

InterContinental Hotels Cultivates Customer Web Community to Improve Business

The world's largest hotel company, InterContinental, is using a private online community to tap into the needs and desires of its most lucrative customers.

Staying abreast of travel and hotel trends and keeping customers happy is an ongoing pursuit for Ken Bott, director of IHG's global consumer marketing group. Bott is highly animated when he talks about the . . . Priority Club Rewards Private Online Community [which] consists of 300 of IHG's most loyal U.S. customers who travel for business at least 15 times a year and tend to fetch up across IHG's hotel chains, as the occasion dictates.

Bott says that staying in close touch with customers, especially the three and a half million most loyal ones, is his priority. The focus group, the traditional method for soliciting feedback from customers for promotional campaigns or hotel-design changes, is a slow and costly method that only generates qualitative results . . . A single study could take three weeks to prepare and cost $10,000, says Bott.

So when IHG began experimenting with online community software, Bott leapt at the chance to set up a focus-group alternative. His group chose a Web-based tool from Communispace, a Watertown, Mass. software company that builds private online communities . . . Communispace was easy to use, Bott says, and had a track record with *Fortune* 50 companies. It took about three months to customize the software to meet IHG's specifications.

It was important for IHG's marketers to receive feedback from customers in as many formats as possible. To that end, customers can provide opinions, suggestions and ask questions in five different ways, including via surveys, chat rooms and topic-specific discussion areas. Surveys focus on the needs and experiences of customers and can accommodate multiple choice responses or open-ended answers. For example, one survey asked members about their

(continued)

behavior when entering a hotel room for the first time. Some wrote that they take off their shoes and get comfortable, while others said they scanned the room from the doorway in search of an Internet connection and outlet for their laptop.

Though such comments are qualitative, Bott says enough respondents expressed a desire for easy-to-find Internet access that the company has selected a couple of pilot hotels in the Atlanta area to experiment with a revised room design; it will have a new orientation for electric outlets and a clear view of the desk chair from the doorway—designs approved by the online community.

There is also a "brainstorming" area of the site where customers can respond to questions from the marketing staff in open text fields. One day, the following question was posed: What do you do with your loyalty club card? More than 50 percent of respondents said it was a hassle to carry around so many cards and that they often left them at home, consequently missing out on earned car rental or hotel points.

Within a few days of the brainstorming session, Bott's team had developed a solution to ease the frustrations of its customers: a rewards card with space on the back for numbers of other hotel, airline and rental-car loyalty programs. Designers built prototypes of the new card and posted them in the private online community to gauge the opinions of customers. Participants favored one design that was eventually produced and mailed out. The whole process—from initial query on the site to card distribution—took four weeks.

Then there is the savings. Where focus groups cost tens of thousands of dollars and only reach a dozen or so customers at a time in a single city, it now costs IHG just hundreds of dollars to send out an email to customers across the country inviting them to take a survey.

Bott says the site isn't all about what customers can do for IHG, but mostly about what customers can do for each other. Community members initiate two-thirds of conversations on the site, he says, mostly related to travel tips, recommendations and questions like where they might find the best pet-friendly hotels. People do occasionally complain about poor service and if there are consistent negative reviews Bott's staff might escalate the complaint.

So much information gets posted on the site that each week one of the marketing staffers consolidates the feedback and emails the information to the whole department along with a synopsis for the chief marketing officer. In 2008, the marketing team will implement a collaborative wiki on the company intranet, which will allow the staff to post observations and analysis about the customer findings, says Bott.[a]

a. Elizabeth Bennett, "InterContinental Hotels Cultivates Customer Web Community to Improve Business," Baseline, January 4, 2008, http://www.baselinemag.com/c/a/projects-Customer-Service/InterContinental-Hotels-Cultivates-Customer-Web-Community-to-Improve-Business/.

tools, all these carefully planned facilities and processes for putting customers to work would go for naught.

Customers understand that IKEA's lower prices do not reflect poorer quality of design or materials. Instead, they believe that their own contribution to the process helps save money; so by transporting and assembling their new furniture, they are helping create their own value. At the same time, they may be adding meaning to the overall customer experience: assembling an end table herself may create an extra sense of value for an IKEA customer.

Other companies have emulated IKEA in inviting customers to create personal value. As we will see in greater detail later, this is especially true at Build-A-Bear Workshop®, where young Guests work with Bear Builder® associates to create and name their own teddy bears and other stuffed animals, then customize the animals' birth certificates with detailed personal information. Beyond absorbing some of the operating costs, these customers contribute to their own customer value equations, helping create experiences that they and their loved ones treasure.

WHY CUSTOMERS WORK

The customer value equation highlights a number of scenarios for putting customers to work in shaping their own experience with your product or service offering.

First, customers are willing to contribute effort when the results are personally important. We see this in the Shouldice Hospital example, where patients' involvement in their own recovery shortens recovery time. When the goal is to enjoy a meaningful, personalized experience, as at Build-A-Bear Workshop, it is easy to get customers involved.

High levels of uncertainty combined with personally important outcomes create conditions in which customers willingly agree to take part in the process. This probably explains why patients are particularly good at self-administering painkillers.

When they want more control over their overall experience, customers generally agree to participate. An increasing number of airline passengers, for example, are willing to check themselves in at self-service kiosks, displacing effort otherwise required of airline employees. Self-check-in has certain advantages, such as viewing available seats, which aren't readily visible when passengers are assisted by an airline agent.

Community (peer) pressure or obvious mutual benefits may encourage customers to participate, for example, in contributing to the quality of an information service such as Wikipedia or Angie's List. This effect is probably also at work when patients agree to counsel other patients at Shouldice Hospital.

In some cases, customers prefer to do themselves what others appear unable to accomplish dependably. For example, delivery services often damage the furniture they handle, either in transportation or assembly. IKEA customers realize that they can probably do a better job than a hired delivery or assembly service, so they willingly roll up their sleeves.

Customers also work for clear, immediate cost savings. That's why many pump their own gasoline in self-service lanes or willingly help clean up trash before leaving a discount airline's plane. Moreover, if human interaction is either unimportant or undesirable, as is the case at many service stations, customers see little downside in serving themselves. Self-checkout lines in many retail outlets take advantage of this trend.

When two or more of these factors are in play, customers recognize the benefits of taking responsibility for tasks that would otherwise fall to the seller. Unfortunately, there are other, less positive situations in which customers put themselves to work, as some businesses learn the hard way.

MINIMIZING NEGATIVE CUSTOMER WORK

Customers may have negative reasons for their brand-related efforts. In fact, alienated customers can work especially intensely and emotionally to detract from the image of a product or service. Research has shown that a satisfied customer typically tells five others of his good experience, but a dissatisfied customer may tell ten or more.[7] More recent studies suggest that the negative effect may be even more pronounced in the highly charged world of networking on the Internet.[8]

We refer to the most disgruntled customers as antagonists.[9] It's especially important to understand how they become antagonists so that you can devise remedial strategies. Sometimes customers are disappointed when you fail to meet their expectations, when in fact those expectations fall outside your strategic value vision. In such cases, it should be easy for employees to recognize that the customer is not a part of your target market and gently explain as much to avoid further misunderstandings. This is what ING Direct does when it needs to "fire" a customer to reinforce its market focus. Its employee owners help unhappy customers understand why there is a disconnect between what they seek and what the company provides. Every outstanding service provider that we've studied has a similar process for disengaging from negative customers to avoid ill will.

Turn Antagonists into Owners

In the best cases, the seller's response to unhappy customers can actually create a new sense of loyalty. For example, well-designed product warranties or service guarantee programs put potential antagonists to work by inviting them to point out problems in the customer value equation as they've experienced it. Implementing a smooth, relatively painless recovery process, fostering an attitude of trust toward customers, and giving employees the latitude (within limits) to take quick corrective action can make all the difference. In fact, such dramatically positive remedies can turn potential antagonists into customer owners.

Catalog and online retailers live or die by their ability to develop high levels of trust in customers' minds. That's why they offer highly effective product and service guarantees. One of the early, successful practitioners of the process is Lands' End, a mail-order retailer. Its unconditional guarantee states, "If you're not satisfied with any item, simply return it to us at any time for an exchange or refund of its purchase price. We mean every word of it. Whatever. Whenever. Always. But to make sure this is perfectly clear, we've decided to simplify it further. Guaranteed. Period."[10] This helps explain why Lands' End is a leader in customer satisfaction among direct retailers.

DESIGNING JOBS FOR CUSTOMERS, CHOOSING THE BEST CANDIDATES, AND MANAGING THEIR WORK

Before you put customers to work, you should clarify your reasons for doing so. Is it to promote your product or service? Is it to reduce your costs? To track your performance? To elicit suggestions for product or service improvements, or for entirely new offerings? To recruit champions who will engage other potential customers?

Each of these objectives requires a different set of actions, with different organizational implications. For example, although your marketing function may be most interested in promoting products or services, operations may be most interested in reducing costs, and business development most interested in the development of new products and services. So it is important to obtain early agreement on the objectives for such initiatives.

Once you've established your objectives, which customers will you choose to put to work? Experience has shown that not all customers are interested in expending effort. So how should you select the ones who are best suited for the job? In fact, you may not have to do so; more often than not, customers select themselves into ownership roles.

The prime candidates may be those who are already most engaged with the brand, product, or service. Others may respond to incentives or to the attractiveness of the jobs you design for them. In either case, you need to orient and train the customers.

Most customer work requires intense communication, so you need to design ways to amplify the voice of the customer. What kinds of listening and response mechanisms will you design? In particular, when your system generates constructive complaints, what kind of recovery processes will you put in place?

Train (or Retrain) Customers

Customers who have not been trained to assist in the work of the organization are most likely to become antagonists. For example, one key part of the strategic value vision at Southwest Airlines is its open-seating boarding process, in which customers line up in a "musical chairs" competition for the best seats. Those familiar with the first-come, first-served process tend to be most willing to tolerate it. They arrive early at the gate and are willing to wait in line, whereas the uninitiated grouse about "cattle car" treatment. Instead of allowing themselves to be trained, unhappy customers may go to the Southwest Airlines Internet gripe site and vent their complaints.

Once trained, even the most loyal customers may be difficult to retrain. For example, Southwest recently introduced a procedure for customers to reserve a place in the boarding lines, either online or at the check-in counter. Media reports suggested that the new process would eliminate the open-seating tradition. To dispel the confusion, the airline established an online "Boarding School" to retrain passengers and explain how to take advantage of the new features. Its Web site poses the question, "Does this mean I have an assigned seat?" and responds, "No. At Southwest Airlines, we believe the best way for you to like where you sit, is to sit where you like. Once onboard, simply choose any available seat . . . and relax."[11] Each "graduation certificate" the Boarding School issues signifies another customer retrained.

Amplify and Respond to the Customer's Voice

Technology has made it easier to track customers' opinions. France Telecom may have been first to recognize the phenomenon, when it introduced Minitel, the first electronic phone book, in 1982. Millions of French subscribers began using Minitel as a way of communicating their thoughts and ideas to tens of thousands of goods and service suppliers. A quarter of a century later, technology offers endless opportunities for listening and responding to customers.

Best practitioners of the craft use customer support centers (not call centers) to ensure that they treat customers like owners. To the extent possible, this requires creating the following:

- A single collection point for complaints and suggestions

- Rapid response

- Latitude for employees to tailor responses for specific customers and situations

- Systems for tallying, tracking, and reporting trends in exchanges with customers

- A clear path for escalating selected messages to other parts of the organization

- Post-response follow-up to determine customer levels of satisfaction with the process

IDENTIFYING POLICY ISSUES: WHAT CAN GO WRONG AND WHAT TO DO ABOUT IT

Beware the law of unintended consequences! Misguided efforts to put customers to work can communicate mixed messages and trigger resentment instead of loyalty. That's why it's important to establish your objectives early, obtain top management support, and adhere to rigid standards in implementing your customer ownership initiative. Above all, follow through when customers agree to contribute to your efforts.

We've identified several sources of trouble and ways to deal with them.

Putting Marketing First

Many organizations assume that they should automatically put marketing in charge of their efforts to put customers to work. But often, the marketing mind-set assumes that the key objective is to control customers' attitudes and actions, something that knowledgeable practitioners see as impossible to do successfully over the long run. Worse yet, the typical attitude that marketing "owns" relationships with customers can end up sabotaging other efforts to enhance the customer ownership quotient.

You saw earlier that various objectives for involving customers require different efforts. So even though marketing may want to elicit referrals from customers—in part because the payoff seems more immediate and understandable—other initiatives may contribute far more value in the long run. For example, operations may want to solicit customer feedback on product or service quality. IT may want to build online customer response systems. Human resources may prefer to invest in perfecting the interface between employees and customers. All these objectives may be more valuable in increasing your ownership quotient than asking customers to help market your products and services.

It's easier to figure out the right objectives if you've identified the kinds of deep indicators for your business that we discussed in chapter 3.

When you've done so, you can choose the types of customer involvement that will produce the greatest long-term impact on your customer ownership quotient. But because many companies are resistant to the idea of ceding control to customers, it takes top management buy in to identify and build effective programs around deep indicators.

Failing to Adhere to Rigid Standards

Pete Blackshaw has identified six deep indicators of brand credibility that apply to any effort to put customers to work.[12] They are trust (confidence, consistency, integrity, and authority), authenticity ("as advertised"), transparency ("no secrets"), affirmation (playback, reinforcement), listening (empathy), and responsiveness (follow-up).

Many companies establish rigid standards and procedures for reinforcing credibility. Unfortunately, many of them have trouble adhering to them consistently, for a number of reasons.

First, the marketing mentality often takes over, especially when customer-generated media reflect poorly on a company's product or service. Management succumbs to the temptation to influence customer feedback or even to suppress unfavorable feedback. This practice destroys trust and authenticity and compromises the entire effort.

Second, management may not have the mechanisms in place to collect and respond to customer feedback from multiple channels. Like most organizations, Toyota receives feedback in a number of ways, including Web sites, word of mouth, and data collected by dealers. The company has made a careful effort to aggregate this input in places where employees can locate and act on it.

Third, even with listening posts in place, management may not pay attention to the feedback customers offer. Doing so requires an openness to the messages customers wish to convey, an attitude that may not be fostered by the organization's leadership. Software developers understand instinctively how to incorporate user input, and some are taking the practice with them as they leave the industry to strike out on new ventures. For example, one of us recently experienced the beta test by the makers of TCHO chocolate, a group of former Silicon Valley software engineers. TCHO's message, which accompanies the chocolate (which is packaged in brown wrapping paper), entices early visitors to the TCHO.com site with this invitation:

> Taste Makers Arise! Come to our website to become an inaugural TCHO Club Member and register your taste feedback. Your opinion will be used to fine-tune tomorrow's chocolate.[13]

Finally, even the highest level of listening is compromised if you fail to follow through on what you hear. At its most basic, follow-through involves acknowledging the suggestion or complaint. Our research suggests that fast, informal, customized acknowledgment is the most effective. But almost any kind of response is better than nothing. Of course, the best outcome from following through on customer feedback may be to make a significant change in your product or service.

Failing to Establish Clear Recovery Processes

The time-honored practice of compensating for problems by offering discounts or free services may not be the most effective way to deal with dissatisfied customers. Instead, as mentioned earlier, a well-defined recovery process can offer better ways to avoid antagonizing customers. Knowing what they can do, when, and for whom helps employees determine what is appropriate in a given crisis. That's why we stress the importance of latitude within limits for employees, a matter we discuss at greater length in chapter 5.

Depending on the degree of ownership among employees, they may need more or less explicit limits. Such limits may involve the expenditure of a specific amount on behalf of a customer or the use of judgment, such as "whatever is reasonable." The latter may vary greatly from one customer to the next, but it requires that you know your customer and his buying habits.

TARGETING THE RIGHT LEVEL OF OWNERSHIP

The customer OQ at eBay is one of the highest we've seen: at least figura-tively, the users own the company. But it hasn't been an easy relationship. eBay's management has had to learn over time just what it means to be owned. For example, it means not making any seemingly minor change to the Web site without consulting users and assessing their willingness to support the change. The company may well proceed against its users' wishes, but at least management knows what kind of reactions to expect.

Karmaloop, too, has a high customer OQ. But as you saw earlier, Greg Selkoe and his team still maintain control over the choice of customer designs to produce.

What is the right degree of ownership to target for your organization? How much control will you delegate to customers for functions like sales and new product development? Are there limits to the benefits of cus-tomer ownership?

Coupling Ownership and Innovation

Opinions differ about the utility of relying on customers for new prod-uct or service ideas as opposed to improvements in existing products or services. For example, Sony for many years under cofounder Akio Morita spurned formal marketing research in designing and developing new products. Nevertheless, managers throughout the company spent a great deal of time observing people and their interactions with various enter-tainment devices. These observations have generated the ideas for some of Sony's most successful products. But its leadership has maintained close control over the product development process. Although Morita acknowledged that the company, while under his leadership occasionally invited small groups of potential customers to review proposed products, few Sony customers are conscious of having been a part of any product development effort.

Compare this approach with Intuit's, which deliberately includes customers in the product improvement process, perhaps as a legacy of the industry tradition that asks customers to help debug defective software products. Customer ownership has been critical to the firm's development. Intuit trains its customer service staff to listen for software update possibilities as they work on solving customers' problems. As a result, each year Intuit adds more than a hundred changes to each of its personal financial software updates. Intuit regards customer service not as a cost center but as a function that pays for itself.

Most of the companies we've described have some kind of customer forum or council from which they get feedback regarding new initiatives. EMC, the world's leading developer and provider of information infrastructure technology and solutions, convenes its customer council regularly. According to Frank Hauck, executive vice president of Global Marketing and Customer Quality, "We regularly bring together thirty to fifty of our top customers—both within the United States and internationally—to help guide our product and solutions development efforts as well as our go-to-market efforts. This is an all-encompassing approach—from brainstorming high-level ideas to prioritizing specific features on our near-term confidential product roadmaps. EMC's customer and partner councils are intended to empower the attendees to provide candid feedback on what's working and what's not. In this way, our customers become our business partners in developing solutions that truly meet their most pressing business needs."[14]

Taking the Customer's Point of View

Every organization must assess how much help it wants from customers who might be able to see around corners. One way to explore the most desirable type and degree of customer input is to ask yourself the kinds of questions customers ask in deciding whether they want to behave like owners. Here are examples.

- What's in it for me?

- Will I see immediate benefits from my efforts?

- Is there a quid pro quo, whether a reciprocal favor or future form of payback, that I can expect from my efforts?

- Is the product or service important enough to me to warrant my taking time to help improve it?

- Do I have a sufficiently favorable view of the organization to help it market its products or services?

Organizations seeking to improve their customer ownership quotient must be willing and able to facilitate the right level of customer involvement. Our work has convinced us that this is possible only if you choose and nurture employees who also think and act like owners. We turn to them next.

Boost Your Employee OQ

Ahealthy OQ among employees is a prerequisite for building your customer OQ. That's the primary tenet of the service profit chain, which maintains that employee satisfaction, loyalty, commitment, and ownership help foster similar attitudes in customers, leading directly to growth and profitability.[1] So even though a relatively small group of customer owners contributes disproportionately to financial performance, your target employee OQ should approach 100 percent.

When we speak of employee ownership, we mean identification with the organization that is so strong that it leads employees to want to make it both a better place to work and a more successful business. Employees may be loyal if they are generally satisfied with their jobs. But until they begin offering meaningful ideas about how to improve their jobs, and until they recruit high-potential friends, they haven't become true owners. When they do, a high employee OQ can produce remarkable results, as we've seen repeatedly in organizations such as Baptist Hospital, Inc. (BHI), the Malcolm Baldrige National Quality Award winning subsidiary of Baptist Health Care based in Pensacola, Florida; Fairmont Hotels & Resorts; Wegmans Food Markets; and SAS.

The Bright Ideas program at Baptist Health Care originated in the hospital's continuous quality improvement initiative. Bright Ideas solicits and implements innovative suggestions for improvement from people at all levels of the organization. Leaders track each idea to completion. Monthly celebrations, hosted by a senior executive, are held to honor all implemented ideas. Leaders receive monthly reports on the number of ideas submitted, under consideration, and implemented as a percentage of full-time-equivalent employees. The number of implemented ideas serves as a metric in annual performance evaluations.

In its first five years, the Bright Ideas program implemented more than twenty-five thousand ideas, representing more than $20 million in annual savings. More important, employees began to express their enthusiasm for working at Baptist Health Care by tracking the number of their ideas that have been put into practice. The sense of ownership is palpable at BHC. Employees even wear T-shirts announcing "I Own Baptist Hospital" or buttons proclaiming "Owner for [x] Years."

Fairmont Hotels & Resorts also has a high employee OQ, in part because its culture makes employees feel like winners when they help their customers win. At the end of each year, the company gives out its Ideas Count awards. To earn them, employees post hundreds of ideas each year on the company's Web site, suggesting ways to improve both the way they work and the value they offer for customers.

One frontline employee, who had noticed guests talking about pets they had left behind, proposed the idea of having a "hotel dog" that guests could walk after a long day of meetings. Enter Morgan, the hotel dog, who comes to work every day with an employee at The Fairmont Waterfront hotel in Vancouver. When Morgan garnered publicity throughout North America, including on popular TV shows such as *Good Morning America*, Fairmont's other hotels began to offer hotel dogs. Competitors soon took up the idea, too.

But Morgan's true value to Fairmont's OQ comes through in a letter that the Fairmont Copley Plaza Hotel in Boston received recently. It read, in part, "We come back every year, and we love Katie Copley [the Boston hotel's dog]. We just got a new 13-week-old Labrador retriever, and we didn't know what to name our dog. So, we want you to know that we named him Fairmont."[2]

Think of the potential for customer ownership resulting from an act of employee ownership. Potential guests, when introduced to Fairmont (the dog), act on the recommendation for Fairmont (the hotel) that accompanies the introduction. And as for Katie Copley, she became the star of a new children's book in 2007. With all the makings of a classic, *Katie Copley* (the book) describes a lovable black Labrador whose job is to walk the guests at the Fairmont's Copley Plaza Hotel in Boston.[3] It is quite likely a gift that will continue giving to the hotel for some time to come.

Wegmans Food Markets, an award-winning New York–based regional supermarket chain, and SAS, a $2 billion developer of corporate software solutions, regularly appear among the best places to work in *Fortune* magazine's annual poll. If *Fortune* had a similar survey among customers for the best places to do business, we'd bet that both companies would appear at or near the top of that list, too. In fact, if you ask Danny Wegman what makes for a successful store, he will tell you, "Happy people." Ask him what else is important and he says, "Happy people, period."[4]

If you visit the SAS Web site and click the tab "Work Life," here's what it says: "If you treat employees as if they make a difference to the company, they will make a difference to the company. That's been the employee-focused philosophy behind SAS' corporate culture since the company's founding in 1976. At the heart of this unique business model is a simple idea: satisfied employees create satisfied customers."[5]

It's striking, when we listen to executives from these organizations, to notice how similar they are in their views about how they compete. Yet one delivers world-class medical care, another offers incomparable experiences in the crowded hotel industry, and still another sells the world's most advanced business intelligence software. And another is about "helping you make great meals easy" in the retail grocery industry.

How do they describe what employees value in a job? They tell us a number of things, including these basics:

- A boss who's fair (who makes the right decisions in hiring, recognizing, rewarding, and firing employees)

- The opportunity to learn and develop personally

- The excitement of working with winners (winners like to work with winners; losers like to work with winners; winners don't like to work with losers)

- Reasonable compensation

And right up there with the others is the opportunity to deliver results to customers, the ability to succeed, or "win," for and with them. People get tremendous satisfaction from being able to do this. Turning employees into winners requires the right training, the right tools and support systems, and the right workplace design. It requires sufficient latitude (within limits) in how they do their jobs. And the implied trust that goes with latitude adds another source of satisfaction—one that helps convert winners into owners.

UNDERSTANDING THE EMPLOYEE VALUE EQUATION

In previous chapters we define the value equation for customers. Similarly, we can construct an employee value equation:

$$\text{Value for Employees} = \frac{\text{Capability to Deliver Value for Customers} + \text{Quality of Work Life}}{[1 \div \text{Total Income}] + \text{Access Costs}}$$

PrairieStone Pharmacy, whose customer value equation we describe in chapter 3, goes further in creating value for employees than the typical pharmacy. In particular, it concentrates on inflating the numerator of the equation. For example, the opportunity to spend time getting to know their customers and their needs enhances PrairieStone pharmacists' ability to deliver results. It also translates into a high-quality workplace, resembling a doctor's office more than a pharmacy. It's not cluttered with stacks of shelves or people tripping over each other filling prescriptions. In short, the job corresponds more closely to what pharmacists expected when they elected to enter the profession.

PrairieStone Pharmacy's employee value equation looks something like this:

Employee Value Equation =

$$\frac{\text{Capability to Deliver Value for Customers}\ (\text{more time with customers, accurately filled prescriptions, packaging that encourages correct consumption, more drugs available on site})\ +\ \text{Quality of Work Life}\ (\text{doctor's office ambience, no clutter, no confusion, ability to be a clinician})}{[1 \div \text{Total Income}]\ (\text{market-rate pay})\ +\ [\text{Access Costs (conveniently located pharmacies)}]}$$

The denominator of this equation may appear to be short on benefits. But if that's the case, why doesn't PrairieStone have a problem staffing its pharmacies? John Brady, cofounder and executive vice president, provides insight here: "You know, we've offered pay incentives, and I'll be honest, the pharmacists really weren't motivated much by them. It's funny, because we thought we knew what would be interesting to them. But the reality was, 'Hey, just let me practice pharmacy. Let me take care of customers.'"[6]

In other words, PrairieStone employees enjoy market-rate compensation and easy access to the workplace, but Brady and his colleagues realize that what really makes their employees happy is the stuff that falls in the numerator of the employee value equation.

If the capability to deliver value in a quality workplace is important to employees, if that's what makes them feel like winners and owners, then we should understand how to make it happen. That means building what we call a cycle of capability.

CREATING A CYCLE OF CAPABILITY

Although every organization has its own approach to management, there are remarkable similarities in the ways that the outstanding performers in our sample make sure that employees win by delivering value for customers. They include the following:

- Careful selection, and self-selection—primarily for attitude—of employees as well as customers

- Clear orientation to company values

- Training for skills and broader personal development

- Support systems that create winners

- Latitude within limits to deliver value to targeted customers

- Measurement, reward, and recognition for delivering value

- Suggestions for new processes and products

- Referrals of others who can help improve the business

Collectively, these efforts produce the kind of loyalty that leads to higher productivity, lower costs, greater satisfaction, commitment, and a sense of ownership for employees and customers alike. Figure 5-1 depicts this as a *cycle of capability*, which creates the essential links between the employee value equation and the customer value equation. In so doing, it cements the relationship between employees and customers by delivering real value for both groups.

Scott Cook, then CEO of Intuit, expressed the philosophy most eloquently to us years ago when he was getting his company off the ground: "Offering customer service only occupies part of somebody's brain. We want to be able to occupy all the mental energy of all the folks in tech support. When they know they are not only solving the customer's problem, but figuring out how to make it so this problem never occurs again,

FIGURE 5-1

Fostering employee ownership: The cycle of capability

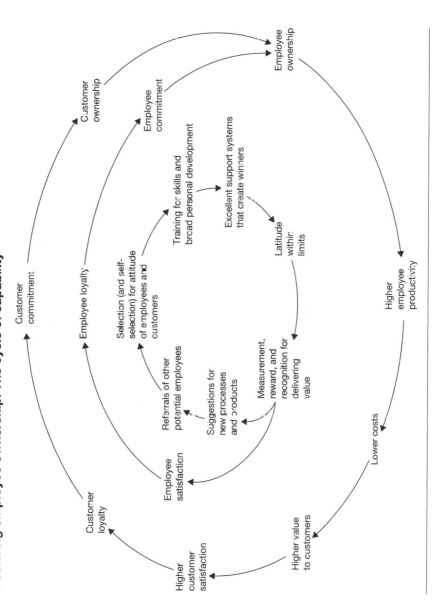

the job becomes more fulfilling. Nobody wants to work in an environment in which all they do is handle complaints. They want to make change happen. They want to make the world better for themselves and their customers. Most companies don't allow this change process to occur, or, if they do, it's so hard that people give up."[7]

As Danny Wegman, CEO of Wegmans Food Markets, puts it, "It's the relationships that always astound me. I see it so often in communications from our customers. For example, a beloved customer may die. The people in the store send cards and sometimes even go to the service. It is just remarkable that the depth of the relationships are such that they go way beyond what anyone would ever dream of."[8]

The steps in creating a cycle of capability seem so intuitively powerful that it's remarkable to us why so few organizations follow them. To be sure, many practice a few or even several of them. But those who implement all of them in sequence are most likely to develop an enduring, self-reinforcing ownership culture. Let's explore how the companies we studied do just that.

Hire for Attitude, Orient for Values, and Train for Skills and Personal Development

In earlier chapters we emphasize the importance of targeting the right customers and training them to understand and participate in your strategic value vision.

Choosing and training the right employees are at least as important— and usually more important. In fact, these first steps are the most critical in creating a cycle of capability. They ensure that all your employees understand, feel enthusiastic about, and take pleasure in delivering the kinds of value you offer for customers. Yet many organizations delegate the task of hiring to those who are not fully qualified to carry it out. This practice may create a false sense of economy, but actually it's a case of "pay me now or pay me later." As Richard Fairbank, CEO of Capital One, points out, "At most companies, people spend 2 percent of their time recruiting and 74 percent managing their recruiting mistakes."[9]

Hire for Attitude. Danny Wegman explains why his company hires for attitude and trains for skills: "We look first for people that have caring qualities. We think that our training and development program can help them to learn particular techniques and skills, but if they don't have qualities like compassion, caring, and enthusiasm, they're probably not going to make it here."

Most of the organizations in our study don't need to find potential owners as employees; potential owners find them. The companies need only decide which ones to select, and they use various tactics to do so. Here are several of them.

- *Candidate screening with research-based tools:* Every company in our study uses some combination of assessment instruments to screen for potential owners and refines the instruments continuously. "Creating 'Owners' at Fairmont Hotels & Resorts" describes how research-based screening works to identify potential owners at Fairmont Hotels & Resorts and also illustrates the entire cycle of capability in this organization.

- *Panel or group interviewing:* At Build-A-Bear Workshop®, if you are interested in being a frontline Bear Builder associate, there is a good chance that you will go through an "audition" along with about five to ten other candidates. The search is for prospective associates who can get acquainted with and entertain Guests. They have to be able to create the unexpected extra touches that produce customer delight. The audition is held in front of operating management and may include a current Bear Builder associate. We found similar group interviews being held in several of the organizations in our study. Even customers have been involved in the process.

- *Realistic job previews:* At Harrah's Entertainment, before receiving a job offer, candidates spend approximately an hour with a high-performing employee holding a similar job. The idea is for the candidates to see both the upside and the downside of the positions they are considering so that they can make as informed a decision as possible before accepting the job offer.

- *Employee self-selection:* Most of the leading firms we have observed encourage employee self-selection. This requires brutally frank information about the job, particularly in organizations that are perceived, correctly or incorrectly, to be operating in "glamorous" industries.

Creating "Owners" at Fairmont Hotels & Resorts

Fairmont's Service Plus strategy represents the company's philosophy and framework for developing a culture dedicated to creating memories for its guests and has earned the recognition of being an employer of choice. There are four key elements to Service Plus: Select the Best, Lead with the Best, Train and Develop, and Recognize and Reward:

1. **Select the Best:** Like all service profit chain leaders, Fairmont begins by paying careful attention to who they attract and hire. Carolyn Clark, senior vice president of human resources, worked with the Gallup organization to develop a selection process by interviewing high performing employees including servers, front-desk representatives, and frontline managers to identify what differentiated their best-performing employees from the average performer. Armed with a clear performance model, Fairmont introduced a structured interview guide to help their recruiters screen potential employees who demonstrate both a clear service orientation and a willingness to own responsibility for solving guests' problems without a lot of supervision. The structured interview helps maximize the fit between a new employee's skills and abilities and a job that is right for them.

2. **Lead with the Best:** Sixty percent of all management positions are filled internally, owing in part to the company's commitment to leadership

Orienting New Employees: First Impressions Count. Remember your first day on the job? Was it this year, last year, or twenty years ago? Was it a memorable experience? Well, if you are a full-time employee at a new Wegmans store you will remember it. And if you can't recall all the details, you can always play the DVD you were given at the end of the day.

From the beginning, Wegmans treats its employees the way it expects them to treat customers. The company goes out of its way to make people feel welcome. Its orientation program, called Living Who We Are, instills Wegmans' values and explains the importance of bringing them

development. As CEO Chris Cahill told us, "I don't want our new manager recruits to be 40 years old when they get their first general manager's job. I want them to be a GM in ten years from when they join us. This means getting them moving fast, every twelve to fifteen months. This is succession planning and for me, this is our fuel." Complementing this strong commitment to building broad experience is a leadership training program to help leaders develop the skills to coach and develop employees.

3. **Train and Develop:** Fairmont's investment in education begins with orientation training and includes technical and interpersonal skills development. All of this is part of a comprehensive career development program.

4. **Recognize and Reward:** Consistent with other firms in our study, Fairmont takes recognition and reward very seriously. One peer recognition tool it uses is called Bravograms, a simple note of recognition from one colleague to another expressing thanks for a job well done. "The power of Service Plus" says Clark, "is that each of the four elements reinforces the other. Individually they are excellent, but together they allow our colleagues to truly turn moments into memories for our guests."

Source: Quotes in this box are from interviews with Carolyn Clark and Chris Cahill, November 2006, Toronto; and author's review of Fairmont Service Plus program information.

to work every day. Six weeks before a new store opens, new hires fly to company headquarters in Rochester, New York, where they're met with big signs: "Welcome to Rochester, Welcome to Wegmans." It's a daylong experience that is videotaped each step of the way. When new employees board the plane for home, they get edited DVDs set to music to take home and show their families.

Danny and Colleen Wegman teach in the program, along with Karen Shadders (vice president of people) and Jack DePeters (senior vice president of operations). Does it make a difference? On its 2006 "Trust Index," which is part of *Fortune* magazine's "Great Places to Work" survey, Wegmans scored 99 percent on the statement, "They made me feel welcomed here when I joined Wegmans."

Baptist Health Care, whose employee OQ we described earlier, organizes a two-day "Baptist Traditions" orientation program. About half of the program is devoted to culture-building activities that emphasize how Baptist employees deliver a better experience for patients. CEO Al Stubblefield explains: "There is a good chance that the service they provided at the other hospital won't cut it here. They need to know that they are about to be held more accountable than they ever have been before. But they also need to know that they will be developed more than ever before."[10]

One of the value statements promoted by the program reads, "Superior service: committed to providing excellent service and compassionate care." A simple gesture has a lasting impact in demonstrating this value for new employees. At the beginning of the program, the administrator of each BHC facility asks everyone to fill out a short form that includes, among other things, their favorite treats. It might be a candy bar or favorite flavor of iced tea. No matter what it is, the next day each person's individual treat is waiting at the end-of-program celebration—a simple message about patient care and personalization.

The opening paragraph of Fairmont's orientation materials for new employees provides a good summary to this section: "Your Orientation marks the beginning of a very special association. You have chosen Fairmont Hotels & Resorts and we have chosen you . . . Our business is about creating memories for our Guests. Your hotel or resort is an integral part of our business so we invite you to make our mission, *Turning moments into memories for our Guests*, your mission."

Training for Skills. The American Society for Training and Development (ASTD) reports that the top firms in its benchmark study spend an average of 2.72 percent of their payrolls on training.[11] It is difficult to compare the firms in our study to this group. By and large, they don't consider training an expenditure; they consider it an investment. As Danny Wegman says, "I have no idea what we spend on training. We don't track it because everything is a learning event for our employees. It's very hard to capture all that. It's not part of our competitive strategy, it is our competitive strategy. That's how we differentiate ourselves in the marketplace."[12]

After returning from Wegmans' new store orientation program, new employees meet with their team leaders to implement their personalized training plans. "Learning Universities" support each of Wegmans' five job families, and a "101" course teaches all employees the basics of food preparation and safety. Depending on the job family, a new recruit goes through a series of learning activities and programs that may even include taking a trip overseas to learn firsthand about the various products offered by Wegmans. In fact, the Wegmans employee advising you on the best cheeses to serve with that $21 bottle of cabernet may have just spent five days in Provence learning firsthand about Provençal cooking and culture. The ultimate purpose of all this training is to create the capability to develop meal solutions to share with customers.[13]

At Rackspace Hosting, training for their unique brand of customer service called Fanatical Support® begins long before employment and extends long after employees come on board, as described in "Training from Pre-employment to University at Rackspace Hosting."

Training from Pre-employment to University at Rackspace Hosting

At Rackspace Hosting, training can begin before employment and continue throughout a person's employment with the firm. It can start with the pre-employment program. Rackspace has used the "Technical Boot Camp" pre-employment training program as a part of the recruiting effort to ensure it ends up with qualified employees that also fit its culture, which is centered around providing "Fanatical Support," the company's term for the kind of customer service it provides. Perhaps a recruit has a basic knowledge of the technical requirements, but doesn't quite understand the company's service philosophy. This is the perfect opportunity for Rackspace to educate her on both professional skills and corporate culture.

The company selects a number of trainees to undergo (typically) ten weeks of paid training focusing on required skills and certifications as well as the corporate culture. Each week, recruits are tested on the training, ending with a final exam. Recruits who make it through the training course, pass each exam, and earn the approval of the trainer may then be offered a full-time position. The goal is to hire approximately 80 percent of the participants.

Fostering Long-Term Employee Development. Companies in our sample enjoy lower turnover than their peers because they foster personal development through challenging job assignments that create career opportunities. For example, at SAS, Vice President of Human Resources Jenn Mann told us: "We're planning to do more with career pathing, to let people know that they can leverage their skills in different areas of the company. For years, we have posted jobs internally so people could self-direct their careers and move around the organization. We would like our employees to have all their careers at SAS."

The same is true at Wegmans. Jack DePeters explains, "We tell people, 'Know how you fit. If you're doing a job and you don't understand how

The new hires then enter Rackspace Rookie Orientation, a four-day in-depth orientation in which new Rackers work in the kind of team environments they will encounter in their jobs. Later, on-the-job training is the order of the day, much of it carried out by the frontline team of which the new recruit will become a member.

In addition to all of this, Rackers have continuing access to role-specific training as well as the courses offered by "Rack U," Rackspace University. Rack U offers technical, managerial, and professional development courses as well as those devoted to teamwork. It also gives Rackers the opportunity to maintain balance in their lives as they grow, by offering personal development courses on top of the multitude of professional courses offered. Some personal development courses have included Yoga, Latin Dancing, Personal Finance, Health and Fitness, How to Buy a House, Fly-fishing, Beer 101, and Fanatical Parenting.

Rackspace University's budget for 2006 was over $2 million for annual training, and every Racker was allotted approximately $3,000 per year for training, beginning the day they were hired. This equates to approximately sixty hours of training annually per Racker.

Source: Authors' interviews with managers at Rackspace Hosting.

it's bringing value to our customer, then find out. If it's not bringing value, then do something different.'"

Career development is as much about moving across the organization as it is about moving up the corporate ladder. As Frank Hauck, executive vice president of global marketing and customer quality at EMC, well known for its information storage and related technology and solutions, puts it: "At EMC it's about being part of something really special. We've created an environment where customers and their needs always come first. We're able to consistently meet, if not exceed, customers' expectations because our employees are empowered to learn—and take action. We pride ourselves on hiring, developing, and retaining the most talented, resourceful, results-oriented individuals we can find. They join us from all over the world. When they join EMC we take the time to assess their skills and immerse them in our technology, business processes, and culture. I think we provide our employees with opportunities for training, education, and professional development they would be hard-pressed to find anywhere else."[14]

Personal development can foster relationships with customers in direct ways. For example, when Wegmans defined its role as solutions provider rather than a grocery store, it assumed responsibility for educating its employees and its customers about cooking and the use of food. This approach has been so successful that a number of customers have come to work for Wegmans—a clear sign of a high OQ.

Select and Train Customers to Enhance Employee OQ

Customers have an important place in the cycle of capability. As we note in chapter 4, it's important to select the right customers and make sure that they understand the kinds of value you intend to deliver. Well-trained customers are more likely to appreciate your product or service offering and participate in creating value. Especially in personal services involving face-to-face service delivery, there is a strong internal reason for selecting customers or encouraging them to self-select: it is the demoralizing effect that abusive customers can have on employees. "Targeting and Training Customers at Mo's Steakhouse" describes one of the more interesting approaches to this challenge.

Design Support Systems for Winners

Support designed to help employees deliver value for customers ranges from good workplace design to high-tech information management systems. Ideally, the support systems free employees from nonwork worries or administrative tasks, guiding them instead in delivering the results customers really value.

Paying Attention to Employees' Needs: Workplace Design. Although we won't attempt to examine all the various dimensions of workplace design, the

Targeting and Training Customers at Mo's Steakhouse

Customers have an important role in creating positive energy at Mo's—A Place for Steaks, founded in 1999 by restaurateur John Vassallo in Milwaukee. Johnny V, as he is known to the local media, has implemented an innovative guest preference software system to identify his most loyal customers and provide them with unprecedented levels of service. There are six customer VIP levels, and any one restaurant can have a maximum of only six (top) "level one" VIPs. You can guess the information Mo's tracks on these VIP customers: their favorite wines, cuts of steak, their spending levels, frequency of visits, and *how well they treat the staff.* Johnny V puts it this way:

> There needs to be a bunch of positive energy and good will in any facility and any business. And I think that we really are working to trade good will. And then we monetize it, right? So here's what I believe. No one keeps negative energy if they can help it. Somebody sits down; they've had a horrible day and they berate a server. Well, it's not like [the server] is going to keep that negative energy to herself. She's going to take that new little present and probably blow it either to another staff member or to a family member later or to a customer. But if the customers are gracious and kind and into the deal and having fun, then guess what? The staff wants to come to work. [a]

Johnny V has taken over two restaurants that failed before his ownership and has made them into thriving enterprises. He combines technology and recommendations from his frontline staff to learn which customers are the best to serve, and—you guessed it—they also turn out to be the most profitable.

a. Interview with John Vassallo, November 2006, Boston, MA.

firms in our sample have taught us a lot about this critical element of support for employees. For example, the SAS campus includes an on-site health care center in a new, state-of-the-art building opened in 2005 with fifty-nine full-time employees. Here, SAS provides medical care, prevention and screening, specialized education, and wellness services (such as nutrition counseling and physical therapy)—all free of charge for employees and their family members. The recreation and fitness center includes a 70,000-square-foot facility containing an eight-lane swimming pool; outdoor jogging trails, tennis courts, softball field, putting green, and multipurpose athletic field; coordinated programs and activities for employees and family members; and paid fitness center memberships for regional office employees. It is staffed with twenty-two full-time employees.

On-site employee services include car detailing, a hair salon, a skin care center, and more, all available at competitive prices. SAS also offers company-sponsored on-site child care for employees' children aged six weeks to five years. The child care program began in 1981 when one pregnant employee faced the choice of being a working or a stay-at-home mom. SAS founders, not wanting to lose the employee's talent and experience, decided they would use one room in a building as a small child care center. The initial enrollment was six children. Now there are more than six hundred children in the program. The cost to employees is $350 per month per child for a service with a market value of approximately $1,200 per month.

Says SAS's Jenn Mann: "SAS treats customers exceedingly well and that treatment extends to our employees because our success depends on how well we develop those long-term relationships. We do everything in our power to make SAS the place you spend the rest of your career. And it's more than programs and buildings; the cultural attitude is that it's okay to take two hours off to see your child's play or go to the gym at 2:00 in the afternoon."[15]

The Wegmans Pittsford store on Monroe Avenue in Rochester, New York, offers a different lesson about figuring out what employees really value. At approximately 140,000 square feet, this store employs almost three times the full-time-equivalent number of employees of its nearest comparable competitor. If you walk through the Pittsford store you see the cheese, bakery, and produce displays staffed by cooking coaches who help customers develop confidence in their ability to pan sear a salmon fillet perfectly.

But in contrast to SAS, there is no day care center. It turns out that Wegmans employees prefer a different kind of support. Jack DePeters explains: "We heard an outcry years ago that people needed day care. So we built a day care center. Monstrous thing, right? State-of-the-art building. I mean we just couldn't have *any* day care center. We had to have the best of the best. [But] nobody went. We couldn't get enough people to go. So then we said, 'That didn't work, so let's put employee day care in a few of the stores.' That didn't work either. What we came to find out was, what the employees really needed, especially for the part-time fathers and mothers, was flexible hours around their day care initiative." So flexible hours replaced day care in the value Wegmans offers for employees.

Implementing Technology: The Double-Edged Sword. Technology-based support systems benefit customers as well as employees. As you saw earlier at ING Direct, such systems facilitate high-speed banking for customers for whom time is valuable. They are at the heart of a high-service, low-cost, customer DIY operating strategy. But the way such systems are used determines their long-term effectiveness and any resulting competitive advantage.

For example, technology can be used to automate tasks so that they get done with little or no human intervention. This application of technology provides little sustainable competitive advantage.

At other times, technology can be employed in the support of humans performing their jobs. Here it may take two basic forms. In one application, it is used to restrict judgment and reduce the scope of employees' jobs as well as the latitude they can employ in carrying them out. This kind of support system requires few qualifications and little training of employees. Jobs are restrictive and boring. What happens? High staff turnover, often to the surprise of companies following this strategy.

Or technology can be used to expand jobs, allowing employees to concentrate on the aspects of the job that require judgment. This latter approach to technology characterizes all of the high-OQ companies we studied.

As you saw in chapter 3, the operating systems at Victoria's Secret facilitate rather than replace employees' judgment. All new frontline store associates, many of them in their first job, learn about the store-level profit model, which outlines important determinants of sales and costs. The model not only describes how Victoria's Secret makes money at the store level but also suggests the quantitative measures on which teams of associates will be recognized and rewarded for their work. Similarly, the ACES labor planning system helps establish basic staffing strategies that managers can alter based on their own judgment.

By using technology to support rather than control employees, all these organizations generate lower rates of employee turnover than their competitors. This is true even at Victoria's Secret, where many first-time employees have little intention to remain very long when they join.

Offer Latitude—Within Limits

Once employees and customers have been hired for attitude, trained for skills, and provided with first-rate support systems, they are ready to be given the latitude to achieve results.

This practice is not about letting everyone run wild. Employees and customers alike need to understand the scope of authority that goes with this latitude. Each of the organizations in our study places a high degree of responsibility on frontline employees to do what is right for customers by assessing situations and using their judgment to decide how to respond. But all subscribe to the theory, backed up by data, that employees and customers nevertheless want to know the limits on employees' authority to act. Some actually set dollar limits for the degree to which employees can compensate a customer in a service recovery issue.

At Ritz-Carlton, for example, employees can spend up to $2,000 on a guest without checking with their managers, should the situation in their judgment require it. At Irving Oil, a regional retailer of petroleum and convenience goods, Senior Operations Manager Al Bugby describes his company's approach: "We've empowered our people to make sure that they feel like they can solve that situation if they're comfortable. If a customer came in with a bad gallon [of milk] that they purchased yesterday, we encourage our associates to not only provide a refund or a new gallon of milk but also a bag of muffins or a box of donuts or a half-gallon of orange juice to take home. Make it differentiated."[16]

EMC counts on employees' judgment in deciding when to ask for authorization. Leo Colborne, senior vice president of global customer service, explains: "There are certainly limitations. I'll give you an example. If we had to charter a flight to ship a box to a location into which we couldn't get a commercial jet, then that would definitely require more than a first-line manager's authorization. But when it comes to shipping parts to an account for spare inventory or shipping an extra body to the account because we want to make sure we have three people there with different skill sets rather than just two, those are all decisions that are made by the frontline technical people without regard for a manager's approval. We trust them in making the right decisions."

Latitude within limits provides the balance to ensure that an organization engineers customer ownership, but not at the expense of shareholders. In fact, we've found that frontline employees use their latitude very carefully and sometimes even too sparingly. But in making the judgments required to exercise latitude, they take on the owner's role.

Aces in Your Places. When given sufficient latitude, frontline employees can devise new methods and achieve remarkable results.

Consider "aces in your places." It's a term we picked up years ago at Taco Bell. The Mexican-themed fast-food chain was experimenting with self-managing teams to run its stores without a manager on-site most of the time. These teams were given responsibility for store opening and closing, selecting new team members, solving problems (including firing), and depositing money in the bank.

The company found that self-managed stores outperformed those with a conventional manager, in both profitability and customer satisfaction. In trying to find out why, Taco Bell's leadership discovered a number of innovative ideas that associates had brought to their jobs. In one case a team was doing something so innovative that it was exported to other stores. It involved team members training each other on jobs on which some members of the team were less accomplished during slack business times. Then when the rush hour began—at, say, 11:30 a.m.—it was "aces in your places." Those who were best at each job assumed "battle stations." Capacity to serve customers was found to increase quickly by 60 percent during these times. When the peak had passed, team members could go back to training each other and carrying out other tasks.

Harrah's applies the same system in its gaming casinos, as described in "Aces in Places at Harrah's."

Aces in Places at Harrah's

When Gary Loveman, CEO of Harrah's Entertainment, and John Bruns, then vice president of customer satisfaction assurance, began analyzing the patterns of customer visits to their company's casinos, they weren't surprised to learn that 85 percent of weekly revenue was produced on Fridays, Saturdays, and Sundays. The weekend was when people liked to gamble. What was surprising were the staffing policies that supported this business pattern. In a 2007 interview with us, Loveman explained:

> Most of our management and our better frontline employees were working weekdays, day shifts, which is precisely when our best customers are not around and we don't make any money. So we introduced "aces in places," the idea of getting the best people when the customers are most active. We thought of it almost like a football cycle, where we play on the weekends, we look at our tape on Monday, see how we played, and everybody gets taken care of by the trainer and we get ready to play again on the weekend. This is the cycle we live all the time. It's a very event-driven business.[a]

So management worked with each property to improve its staffing, scheduling, and time and attendance systems to make sure its best people were scheduled for weekends and its other busiest times.

a. Gary Loveman, interviewed by Earl Sasser, February 2007, Boston.

Measure, Recognize, and Reward Employees in Every Way and Often

All the organizations that we have studied and worked with meet the criteria of fair pay. How each gets there is unique, but all of them customize their employee value equation to fit their business model. Some, like PrairieStone Pharmacy, concentrate on the numerator, whereas others emphasize the denominator.

At one end of the spectrum we see organizations like Harrah's and Irving Oil, which combine competitive wages for frontline service providers and managers with variable pay systems based on store or property performance. Others, like Baptist Health Care, Fairmont Hotels & Resorts, and Wegmans, eschew incentive-based pay but offer attractive salaries along with other kinds of value. In his classic study *Work and the Nature of Man*, Frederick Herzberg argued that the real long-term motivators are the intrinsic rewards, such as meaningful jobs, responsibility, and results.[17]

The right combination of performance metrics and rewards needs to fit the firm's business model and its culture. For example, at Harrah's, CEO Gary Loveman feels strongly about a quarterly customer satisfaction bonus that every frontline employee has the chance to earn. For tipped positions at Harrah's, the monetary reward is much less significant. For employees in those jobs, Loveman says that it's more about the message than the money.

If there is some divergence among our sample companies when it comes to pay systems, there is singular convergence when it comes to recognition programs. Organizations that are developing employee ownership make recognition a new art form. For example, recognition is a constant concern at Fairmont Hotels & Resorts, whose Service Plus program we described earlier. When we talked with Carolyn Clark, senior vice president of human resources, she told us: "We have actually taken our Service Plus recognition program up a notch. In January of 2007 we reenergized our recognition program under the umbrella of Memory Maker. With this program we recognize colleagues who deliver

'Fairmont moments.' We find out 'what is your dream? What memory can we create for you?' Maybe their memory is that they haven't seen their family in Columbia for three years and they want to fly them here. We're going to personalize the memories that we create for our colleagues just like they personalize the memories that they create for our guests."[18] Fairmont recognizes two employees each year at each property with this program, financing $5,000 to help make their dream a reality. One employee winner last year needed a new kitchen floor, another hoped to take her mother to London. Memory Maker made both of these dreams a reality. *BusinessWeek* recently recognized Fairmont Hotels & Resorts as one of their Customer Service Champs 2008.[19] Memory Maker was featured as an example of why they were chosen. "Our guests do not want service that's cookie-cutter," says Clark. "Just as we're trying to deliver individualized, personalized experiences for guests, we wanted to introduce a customized, personalized rewards program for employees, too."

The impact of effective reward and recognition is tangible, visible, and emotional. It is one of the things that service profit chain leaders do best. And we've seen that sometimes the best practices can cost the least.

Capture the Employee Ownership Payoff

Organizations that build a strong cycle of capability generate a surprising number of ideas for everything from new processes and practices to new products or services. They also realize unusually high internal referral rates for potential new hires. For example, we found from our research at Harrah's that there is a consistent correlation between effectiveness at converting new employees (from recommending them to having them join the organization) and the number of product service improvements that are offered. Specifically, an employee that offers six or more product/service improvements, on average, has a 24 percent greater conversion rate of new employees. These are the ultimate signs of ownership and the payoff for organizations that foster it.

Welcoming Ideas and Suggestions. Not surprisingly, the companies we studied implement a high ratio of ideas and suggestions that come from employees and customers—sure signs of a high OQ.

Employee owners advance ideas whether or not they are encouraged. Nevertheless, it helps to provide encouragement and meaningful recognition. The best ideas can be prescient, ultimately producing great sources of value for the company, its employees and customers, and its shareholders. Such efforts can yield ideas for new, profitable products. At Best Buy, for example, the Geek Squad service team devised an external disk drive for PCs, which the company has added to its growing list of house brands.[20]

Encouraging Internal Referrals. Leaders in fostering employee ownership generate many high-quality job referrals from their employees. This is the essence of a high employee OQ and the final link in the cycle of capability.

In some months at Rackspace, the number of new hires referred by current employees exceeds 60 percent. That represents huge savings in terms of recruiting costs. Wegmans regularly hires customers who ask how to apply for jobs after observing how employees treat each other in the stores. But more important, frontline personnel in these organizations are by far the best judges of associates who will fit with the organization.

One caveat, however, is that employees tend to refer those who are most like them. As a result, referrals from the best performers may have to be treated differently from those offered by weaker members of the team.

Avoiding Potential Pitfalls as You Capture the Payoff. Unfortunately, the cycle of capability operates in both directions. Ill-advised management decisions can damage employees' sense of ownership and trigger a similar reversal among customers. Consider what happened at electronics retailer Circuit City recently. In March 2007, the company announced that it would replace 3,400 of its more experienced, higher-paid sales-people with new, lower-paid hires. As one reporter commented, "Too bad that service matters in the . . . retail market. Shoppers quickly noticed and fled—leaving Circuit City's sales and profit plunging. Its same-store (2007) holiday sales . . . fell 11.4 percent. And its stock is now about 80 percent below where it was the day before it made the staffing announcement . . . Customers have posted their frustrations with the retailer on-line, in blogs and chat rooms. Many tell of a noticeable apathy among Circuit City's workers."[21]

HARNESSING THE MIRROR EFFECT

Employees who experience satisfaction, loyalty, and a sense of ownership will engender similar attitudes in customers. Their mutually rewarding experiences produce a mirroring effect that drives positive outcomes for both. (Unsatisfactory interactions can also reverse those outcomes, as you saw earlier.) Although this thinking has provoked controversy among our academic friends, our research reinforces our belief in the mirror effect diagrammed in figure 5-2.

In fact, we have come to believe that if we can measure the levels of satisfaction, loyalty, commitment, and ownership that exist on either side of the mirror, we can predict the levels of the same feelings and behaviors on the other side. Above all, the mirror effect shows that delivering value for customers contributes to value for employees, and vice versa. In short, as our high-OQ organizations understand, the connection between employees and customers can end up making all the difference.

Despite significant advances in self-service technology to deliver more value for customers and shareholders, the leaders in our study maintain that it takes people to create an emotional bond with the customer. Danny Wegman puts it this way: "If you measure the service you get at Wegmans compared to some other place, we always come out pretty good on that. But I think it's gone to a new level. I hear that when folks are in a bad mood, they go to Wegmans to cheer up. People

FIGURE 5-2

The mirror effect: Striving for self-reinforcing ownership behaviors in employees and customers

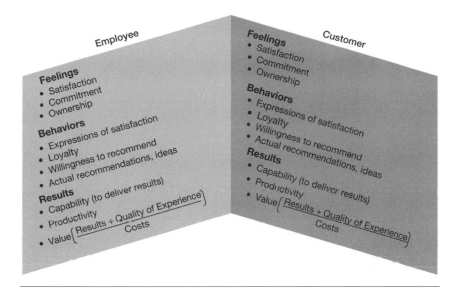

greet you with a smile and ask you if you want a taste of something. Customers get a happy fix and that makes our people feel spectacular. It's circular."[22]

When we asked him about that, Wegman told us that it goes even further. He now sees customers and employees sharing each other's recipes and discussing ideas for using the Wegmans private label products in different ways. This kind of self-reinforcing mirror relationship between customers and frontline employees drives the OQ and acts as a multiplier in delivering financial performance.

The payoff of the mirror effect shows up in various ways. We've talked a lot in this chapter about Fairmont's effort to build employee ownership. One indication of the payoff is that Fairmont was rated third among all firms in the United States in customer service in 2008 in a *BusinessWeek* poll.[23] Fairmont ranked nine places ahead of the Ritz-Carlton organization.

Leaders of organizations mentioned in this chapter have all figured out that they may be in charge of the company, but the employees are in charge of the customer. Jack DePeters, chief operating officer for Wegmans, makes this point most succinctly: "I kid with people that we're a company run by sixteen-year-old cashiers."

LEVERAGING THE CYCLE OF CAPABILITY

With revenues of approximately $2 billion, SAS is a formidable competitor in complex corporate software systems. Its business intelligence solutions foster an ownership attitude among clients by helping them track behaviors and prevent attrition among their own customers. SAS has built a strong cycle of capability and a very high employee OQ.

Vice President Jim Davis makes the company's business case for investing in the cycle of capability, which begins with the financial advantage of low employee and client turnover:

> When you look at the benefits package in terms of how we care for the employee, there is no difference between how we're treating a salesperson, an executive, or somebody who's cutting the grass who's also an employee. We all have the same package. [SAS founder] Jim Goodnight is responsible for this culture. He was a visionary upfront in terms of recognizing if I spend an extraordinary amount of money on making sure my employees have a good work-life balance then it's going to pay off for me in terms of returns with my customers, quality of software, et cetera. So we're running a turnover rate of around 4 percent on an annual basis, where the industry is 18 percent to 22 percent. There have been a couple of studies that look at how much money we save on an annual basis [as a result of high employee loyalty], which they cite as approximately $85 million. I think it's incredibly conservative. You've got six to twelve months before new hires are fully entrenched in your culture and productive. That's really, really expensive.

Davis refers to the financial advantage of higher employee productivity. Previous studies have demonstrated that the top 1 percent of high performers in highly complex tasks demonstrate 127 percent better productivity than average performers.[24] Jenn Mann provides some insight into how this works at SAS: "We encourage collaboration at every level, and there are many ways to go about it. There's a vast repository of knowledge employees can tap electronically to help them do their jobs better. We also have blogs, wikis, e-mail communities, and regularly scheduled knowledge-sharing events. Perhaps more important, we provide many opportunities for employees to network informally in the workplace. An amazing amount of work gets done over lunch in our cafeterias and during pickup basketball in the gym."

Relationships like these that are built up over time—that can achieve deeper and more efficient levels of learning and development—result in better software products. And everything about the SAS business model is designed to foster those relationships by its investments in its cycle of capability.

As you've seen, it can be hard to measure the overall economic effects of investing in the cycle of capability. But when companies enhance employees' ability to deliver value for customers, they invariably increase their ownership quotient among employees and customers alike. And those that are best at fostering ownership learn to practice what we call anticipatory management. Chapter 6 explores how they coordinate marketing, operations, human resources, and information technology to anticipate and meet the needs and expectations of employees, customers, and investors.

6

Engineer Ownership Through Anticipatory Management

Organizations that engineer owner-ship learn to predict and respond to customers' needs before they arise. Technology and information systems can be a great help in this endeavor. But just as important are the combined efforts from all parts of the organization—especially marketing, operations, human resources, and information technology—working seamlessly together to help frontline employees deliver value for customers. Organizations as diverse as Harrah's Entertainment, the New York Police Department, and Build-A-Bear Workshop® have all developed this capability we call *anticipatory management*—and it pays off in the degree of ownership they enjoy.

Reams have been written about one of the most advanced customer affinity programs ever devised. It's called Total Rewards, and it enables Harrah's Entertainment to identify individual behaviors and preferences for 40 million customers. But when Gary Loveman, CEO of Harrah's, gets really excited, it's about harnessing this vast database to turn its casino operations into something he calls an "active enterprise"—one with an entirely new set of coordinated organizational capabilities.[1] Loveman puts it this way:

> The revolution is this: when you check in with us in Vegas or Atlantic City or Tunica, Mississippi, we're going to engage with you in real time during your visit through a digital device to invite you to do things with us based on what capacities we have and what your preferences have been shown to be. So if you're a connoisseur of fine dining and you're in Vegas at any one of our properties, and we have availability at 8:45 p.m. in one of our best French restaurants, we're going to engage with you through that device to encourage you to come see us, to extend your stay a day, to come to a sweepstakes we're running at the Flamingo, or any number of other things . . . We want to engage with you and try to yield-manage the assets and also encourage you to make sure that you consolidate your spending with us, rather than wandering out to the other places.[2]

If you spend fifteen minutes in the slot machine dispatch center of Harrah's Las Vegas, you get up close to the revolutionaries themselves, actively matching organizational capacity with customers' needs. The computer screen being monitored by Stephanie Winslow, Harrah's slot dispatch supervisor, displays the activity of Harrah's guests across a bank of slot machines. At a glance she can tell which guests are Seven Star (the most valuable to Harrah's), Diamond, Platinum, or Gold players. The screen starts flashing, and Winslow moves into action: "Jill, Mrs. Hermes, Diamond player on slot 34, needs assistance." Seconds later Jill responds with two words: "Thirty-four cleared." The screen stops flashing, and Winslow smiles and says, "At Harrah's, Diamond customers are very important."

Compare this story with one Loveman tells about his first night on the floor of one of Harrah's casinos:

> I stopped and asked a gentleman who was playing a slot machine. [I asked him,] "How are you doing tonight, sir?" and he said

"Shitty." It dawned on me that my parents had not taken me through the "How are you—shitty" dialogue. I did not know what to say. The same experience was repeated more than once that night and I found myself not wanting to ask that question any more. But that is the world that my employees live in every day. Providing service in this environment is tricky, because most guests end up losing while playing in a casino. We had not trained our people to deal with these kinds of situations. We wanted to deliver a world class service experience that would transcend this issue.[3]

How Harrah's progressed from this situation to dispatching Jill to serve Mrs. Hermes on slot machine 34 is a remarkable evolution. In some respects, it's similar to the transformation at the New York Police Department, when it reorganized and undertook related initiatives to harness the full power of the CompStat system to enable police officers to anticipate and reduce crime by intervening before it happens, as described earlier.

Building Harrah's immense Total Rewards database and learning to mine its rich lode of information enable Harrah's to anticipate virtually every guest's desires—and customize its services on the spot. As you will see, this capability is particularly valuable in cultivating ownership among the most attractive customers, the Seven Star and Diamond players.

This chapter describes how leaders like Harrah's Entertainment engineer ownership by developing communities of loyal customers, collecting extensive data about them, transforming the data into information that can be used to predict their interests and preferences, and creating a tight cross-functional organization that can act on that intelligence. Anticipatory management brings together the employees who manage marketing, operations, human resources, and information systems and focuses their efforts in a "one firm" approach to delivering value for customers. It uses mechanisms such as cross-functional teams and dynamic delivery systems that coordinate capacity and demand. Put in the right places at the right times, the teams are trained to anticipate and deliver value on a mass customized basis. They do this through carefully developed processes that we characterize with the term *simple excellence*. Employees as well as customers benefit from this set of concepts at the heart of anticipatory management.

Because the elements of anticipatory management are complex and interactive, the stories here are detailed. If you want to get a good idea of how the ownership is engineered, stick with us.

DEVELOPING A COMMUNITY OF OWNERS

Some kinds of businesses, particularly those that are networked, such as telecommunications and Internet-based businesses, offer natural opportunities to develop a community of loyal customers. But this opportunity is no guarantee of success, as demonstrated by the cell phone and cable TV industries, which are high on many people's "most hated" lists.[4]

Communities can develop around shared interests, some as simple as the desire to connect. The Internet has spawned communities ranging from bird-watching enthusiasts to car repair aficionados, bloggers, Scrabble lovers, and the YouTube and MySpace nations. For commercial organizations, the power of networking is the opportunity it gives you to create loyal communities of owners, most often through customer affinity programs. Harrah's Entertainment is a recognized master of this skill.

From Rewards to Ownership at Harrah's Entertainment

When Gary Loveman arrived at Harrah's Entertainment in 1998 as head of operations and marketing, then-CEO Phil Satre and his team had just developed a $17 million computer system to harvest data about the people who visited Harrah's casinos. Whenever a customer requested a membership rewards card, the system collected data such as gender, age, and other nonfinancial demographics. Then whenever the customers inserted their cards into slot machines or handed them to dealers or roulette croupiers, the system tracked the types of games played, playing time, and money wagered. Using their cards allowed customers to earn rewards such as free hotel rooms, dinners, show tickets, and special promotions.[5]

But the program had some problems. As Loveman explains, "First, nothing differentiated this program from our competitors' efforts. Our customers simply took their free rooms and dinners and drifted across the street to do their gambling. Second, our customers earned different rewards at different properties; there was no uniformity in the program. Third and most important, our customers were not given any incentive to consolidate their gaming with Harrah's."[6]

Harrah's simply lacked the talent to take full advantage of its investment in information systems by creating a new way of serving customers. "We were going to move in a direction that required principally two sets of skills that we didn't have in great quantity in the company," according to Loveman. "One was this devotion to service and process, and the second was quantitative marketing. So we had to go out and recruit for skill sets that not only didn't exist in the company, they didn't exist in the industry."

If Harrah's was to realize its potential, it was clear that operations, human resources, and marketing would all play important roles. The three groups would have to cooperate and integrate their efforts to target several specific objectives:

- Rethinking service processes to deliver desired value every time (operations and human resources)

- Consolidating the play of existing customers with service (operations and marketing)

- Growing same-store sales with repeat customers as well as those referred to Harrah's by them, primarily because of loyal, productive employees (human resources)

- Attracting new customers with a newly achieved reputation for delivering value (marketing)

Achieving these objectives would require a new level of cooperation and integration among the three functions, all of which represent critical links in Harrah's service profit chain. Figure 6-1 shows the service profit chain that management created to reflect its strategic value vision.

Customers came to know Harrah's new strategy as its Total Rewards program. But the program was only the tip of the strategy iceberg. As you can see in figure 6-1, Total Rewards represents only one part of an effort to reengineer the company.

Creating a Customer Community from Scratch at Build-A-Bear Workshop

Just a year before Gary Loveman joined Harrah's, Maxine Clark was founding Build-A-Bear Workshop. But unlike Loveman, Clark had the luxury of engineering ownership from scratch. Trained at May Department Stores and Payless ShoeSource and with years of experience in promoting and growing retail operations, she had a clear vision of what the Build-A-Bear Workshop Guest experience should be like and how it should feel. Children and their parents would make their own stuffed animal friend, enjoying a participative experience unlike others they usually shared. This would take place in an interactive process, with the Guests playing the major role in the creation of value, supported by carefully selected and trained Bear Builder associates.

From choosing a bear to making a bear birth certificate, the process enables the company to create emotional bonds with its Guests. At the same time, it compiles a base of willingly provided data, particularly at the Name Me station as described in "The Build-A-Bear Workshop Guest Experience." The information collected there enables Build-A-Bear Workshop to learn all about the new furry friends and their owners who can choose to receive ongoing communications, so Build-A-Bear Workshop can maintain relationships with the families that shop in their stores. The information forms an electronic bond between the brand and each animal's new family. It allows Build-A-Bear Workshop to market directly to its Guests, with their permission, through lower-cost channels such as e-mail and direct mail, with cost-effective incentives for return visits, especially just before the new furry best friend's birthday.

FIGURE 6-1

Harrah's service profit chain, including metrics for each link in the business model

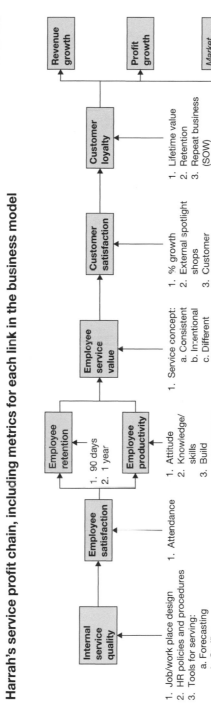

The Build-A-Bear Workshop Guest Experience

Build-A-Bear Workshop was founded as an interactive entertainment retail experience based on the enduring love and friendship that connects us all to stuffed animals, and especially to our teddy bears . . . The teddy bear theme is carried throughout the store with original teddy bear fixtures, murals and artwork. The store associates, known as master Bear Builder associates, share the experience with Guests at each phase of the bear-making process. Regardless of age, Guests enjoy the highly visual environment, the sounds and the fantasy of this special place while they create a memory with their friends and family.

HOW TO MAKE A BEAR AT BUILD-A-BEAR WORKSHOP

Guests who visit a Build-A-Bear Workshop store enter a lighthearted teddy-bear-themed environment consisting of eight bear-making stations.

1. **Choose Me:** At Choose Me, Guests are introduced to the stuffed animals in the store and select one, which soon becomes their new furry friend.

2. **Hear Me:** At Hear Me, Guests may select from several sound chips to place inside their stuffed animal to further personalize their new friend. The sound chip is inserted safely inside the plush during the stuffing process. Guests can also record their own twelve-second Build-A-Sound message.

3. **Stuff Me and Heart Stuff:** At Stuff Me, master Bear Builder associates fill the new friend with stuffing for just the right amount of huggability. A very special step that is unique to Build-A-Bear Workshop also happens at this station. Each Guest participates in the heart ceremony—a Build-A-Bear Workshop trademark—selecting a small satin heart, adding to it his or her own love and wishes, and carefully placing it inside their new furry friend.

4. **Stitch Me:** At Stitch Me, the last seam is neatly pulled shut, nearly completing each new best friend. Before closing the animal, the associate

inserts a barcode, allowing Build-A-Bear Workshop to reunite a lost stuffed animal with its registered owner if it is ever lost and returned to a store.

5. **Fluff Me:** At Fluff Me, the Guest brushes his new best friend at the air bath to make sure it is perfectly fluffed.

6. **Dress Me:** At Dress Me, Guests may dress their new friends in the beary latest furry fashions.

7. **Name Me:** Guests then stop at the Name Me computer, where they answer several questions about their new furry friend, including the birth date and, of course, the name. This information is compiled and becomes part of a personalized birth certificate for the Guest to take home. Guests can select their local language, including English, Spanish, or French.

8. **Take Me Home:** Guests conclude their bearmaking adventure at the Take Me Home station, where they are given their customized birth certificate and can join the Stuff Fur Stuff loyalty club. Each new furry friend is then placed (comfortably, of course) in their very own Cub Condo carrying case, which is designed as a handy travel carrier and new home for their friend.

    buildabearville.com: When Guests get home they can bring their new furry friend to life online to play together in buildabearville.com—their online world stuffed with fun.

BEAR LIFESTYLE AND PARTNERS

Guests are able to express the true personality of their new best friend by choosing from hundreds of outfits and accessories. Build-A-Bear Workshop stays on the cutting edge of furry style by partnering with fashion leaders like Limited Too, SKECHERS shoes, and even bear-sized Major League Baseball, NBA, and WNBA club uniforms, tees, and hats.

Source: Adapted from a Build-A-Bear Workshop *Fact Sheet*, www.buildabear.com.

Clark knew that she was really onto something the moment she opened the doors to her first store in St. Louis in October 1997. The objective was to provide a theme park–like experience in about 2,700 square feet of retail space. From that first store, it was a rapid road to the opening of more than 325 company-owned stores located in the United States, Puerto Rico, Canada, the United Kingdom, Ireland, and France.

Along the way, Build-A-Bear Workshop turned insight into innovation in finding ways to reach its target Guests and expand its customer community, such as offering both electronic and plastic Bear Bucks gift cards that Guests can give to their friends to introduce them to the concept and its community. Some of the best community-building ideas came from the company's commitment to intent listening. It continually asks its young community members what they'd like to see the company do to continue having them as Guests. As Scott Seay, president and chief operating Bear, told us: "Our Guests have always been passionate about our brand, and we get over seventy-five hundred letters and e-mails each month and answer every one of them. When kids started sending in their ideas for clothing designs, we decided to have a design contest for a new outfit for one of our mascots. We've always carried sports gear and outfits for bears, but our Guests wanted the authentic look of their favorite teams so we added licensed uniforms and apparel from the top professional sports leagues. We listen to store location suggestions, new product and store event ideas."

The power of the Build-A-Bear Workshop community manifests itself in Guests' responses to initiatives like the Stuff Fur Stuff club loyalty program, which has over 6 million members. This was particularly significant at a time when competitors were targeting the same customer segment with offerings such as stuffed animals and virtual habitats for them (Webkinz) and virtual Web environments keyed to motion pictures (Disney's Tinker Bell) and social communities (Disney's Club Penguin). The interactive virtual world of Build-A-Bear Workshop—buildabearville.com—quickly grew to more than 4 million virtual online characters within the first six months of its launch on

December 11, 2007. As the only company with both real world stores and an online world, Build-A-Bear Workshop is uniquely positioned and has significant opportunity. For example, following Hannah Montana's "Best of Both Worlds" sold-out concert tour, Build-A-Bear Workshop staged a unique promotion. With a purchase of $15 or more at a Build-A-Bear Workshop store, Guests received a code that allowed them to view backstage footage from the tour in the Pawforming Arts Center at buildabearville.com and receive a virtual guitar for their online characters. In addition, Guests could dress their animals in the latest Disney styles and even purchase the newest music CD in the company's stores. The power of the Build-A-Bear Workshop community of Guests becomes even more accentuated as these Guests participate in buildabearville.com and become even greater owners of the brand.

BUILDING AND SHARING A COMMON CROSS-FUNCTIONAL DATABASE

Maxine Clark envisioned a common cross-functional database for Build-A-Bear Workshop from the start. But at Harrah's Entertainment, Gary Loveman and his colleagues needed to graft such a system onto an existing organization. One of the people Loveman recruited was David Norton, who today acts as Harrah's chief marketing officer. Norton and his team forged a new approach to segmentation, data mining, and direct marketing—one that integrates data from marketing, operations, and human resources in a significant departure from standard practice.

Norton's team found, for example, that only 26 percent of gamblers generated 82 percent of the revenues.[7] Another surprise was that "the company's best customers were not the high rollers that the entire industry had targeted for many years, but rather former teachers, doctors, bankers, machinists, or essentially middle-aged and senior adults with discretionary time and income who enjoyed playing slots . . . These customers didn't value free hotel rooms and didn't typically stay in the hotels, but instead desired free casino chips as rewards, as many of them lived near the casinos they visited."[8]

The team devised a way of estimating the lifetime value of a customer on the basis of individual profiles in the Total Rewards database combined with just a few months' experience of each guest's visits to Harrah's casinos. Over the course of a year, guests' play earns them Total Rewards tier status: Diamond, Platinum, or Gold. Each Diamond represents a lifetime value (approximately $100,000) to Harrah's that is fifty-three times that of a Gold customer and four times that of a Platinum customer, yet Diamonds represent only 5 percent of the total population of customers. (The recently created Seven Star category comprises guests with an annual value of $50,000 or more.)

Norton's team found that customers who had rated Harrah's a B on overall service the preceding year and maintained that B rating the following year demonstrated an improvement in profitability of 10 percent. Since the customer did not perceive a change in the service experience, it was clear that this 10 percent improvement in profitability was attributable to marketing or product enhancements. But those customers that moved their top-box satisfaction rating from a B rating to an A rating also increased their revenue to the company by 22 percent. This incremental 12 percentage point improvement in revenue was clearly attributable to the service experience and helped build the case for developing Harrah's service culture and delivery systems.

As a result of these findings, Harrah's management launched a substantial cross-functional effort to get its operating strategy and value delivery systems right before investing in market development.

COORDINATING OPERATIONS, MARKETING, AND HUMAN RESOURCES TO ACT ON PREDICTIVE INTELLIGENCE

Leaders in engineering ownership use intelligence from their cross-functional databases to design operations that consistently exceed customer expectations. This practice takes expertise in many areas:

- Communicating strategy so that everyone understands why exceeding customer expectations is so important in the first place

- Positioning employees to win in creating results for customers

- Making complex operating systems very simple at the point of execution, thereby freeing frontline performers to focus on customers

- Defining measures, standards, and fail-safe mechanisms that predict performance outcomes before they happen so that preventive action can be taken in real time

- Creating an anticipatory management system that links and helps drive improved value for employees, customers, and investors

Delivering Customized, On-the-Spot Value at Harrah's Entertainment

The operating strategy and value delivery system at Harrah's Entertainment is easily one of the most sophisticated in any industry. It delivers on all five of the imperatives just mentioned.

While the customer relationship management and direct marketing capabilities were being developed, John Bruns, a former Ritz-Carlton executive recruited to lead customer satisfaction assurance, was busy building an operating strategy to delight the customers that marketing would subsequently drive through the doors. Early on, Bruns encountered frustration regarding the methodology for measuring customer satisfaction and the related rewards system.

Managers were working to improve service to move their scores into the highest category (A) on a Targeted Players Satisfaction Survey (TPSS) that Loveman had introduced in order to link bonuses to performance, but their efforts simply weren't moving the needle. One of the problems Bruns's team discovered was that measures were based on a sample selected randomly among all customers rather than one weighted for those with the greatest impact on economic performance. Bruns explains, "One of the first things I did was change the survey methodology so that we had an equal number of Diamonds, Platinums, and Golds [thereby increasing the proportion of Diamonds in the sample]. That gave us an ability to see whether or not our service strategy of differentiating the experience for Diamond customers was making a difference." Top-box A scores began to improve in ways that had the most impact on the bottom line. And managers began to make their quarterly bonuses.

If the marketing communication message to customers was to be "Come to Harrah's to feel exuberantly alive," the customer experience in the casino had to deliver on that promise. The operating strategy at Harrah's centers on a differentiated service experience for *key result customers* (the most valuable) to achieve specific results for each tier of customer across what the company calls *moments of truth*:

- Reservations

- Valet parking

- Total Rewards card center

- Cocktail or beverage service on the casino floor

- Restaurants

- Checkout

For example, at a physical level, key result customers get a separate block of hotel rooms and separate areas (with higher-quality amenities) in Harrah's restaurants. Separate table games as well as other promotions and activities also are reserved for them. At the slot machines, when there is a payout or other activity requiring a response, Seven Star and Diamond customers are always attended to first, even if their event occurs after that of a Gold customer. Key result customers are given small colored stickers to put in their car windshields so that when they arrive, parking valets park their cars close to the casino.

Bruns explains how employees are trained to deliver differentiated service: "We make it very clear to our employees that the focus is on Seven Star and Diamonds. And we show our staff this customer information so they understand their value to our company. We also make it clear that we don't provide poor service to other customer tiers. We have a minimum standard of service that is provided to all customers, which is a very good level of service."

This means that frontline employees must discriminate between customers in an environment in which identifying which customer is a Diamond and which is a Gold is difficult. It's especially hard at times when the hotel and casino are operating at their maximum capacity. To make matters worse, they must do this while following a myriad of regulations on how to interact with customers. For example, in some states employees are required to roll up their sleeves and show their arms to the closest closed-circuit camera after shaking hands with a customer—not exactly standard procedure on most jobs.

The CSA Operating Strategy. To meet the challenge, Bruns led a Customer Satisfaction Assurance (CSA) initiative in developing an operating strategy based on the drivers of customer satisfaction. To illustrate, we concentrate here on the two most important drivers of satisfaction: friendly and helpful service, and wait time. We'll use Diamond customers for our illustration.

To help employees understand how best to create exceptional experiences that exceed Diamond customers' expectations, the CSA team first identified five behaviors important to each moment of truth, which it called the Spotlight 5 (all are components of what has become known as Spotlight on Success). The team described the key behaviors as follows:

- Initiates friendly greeting

- Smiles and makes eye contact

- Demonstrates upbeat and positive attitude

- Checks for satisfaction

- Provides warm farewell

The team defined standards for employees and managers to apply for each of these behaviors during all of the moments of truth.

As it turns out, exceeding expectations in the Spotlight 5 behaviors can increase not only customer satisfaction and loyalty but also revenue. As one case in point, Harrah's has found that high performance on the "demonstrates upbeat and positive attitude" behavior increases customer tolerance for wait time, providing possible economies in operation.

For example, when the standard for the cocktail or beverage service on the casino floor was lowered from fifteen to twenty minutes to "acknowledge the customer" and take a drink order, and from seven to ten minutes for delivering the order, Bruns and his team noticed something interesting. As long as the server remained upbeat and positive, there was no significant change in the customer's level of satisfaction. But when the standard was moved to greater than twenty minutes to acknowledge the customer and greater than ten minutes to deliver the drink, then despite the server being just as upbeat and positive, the customer rated the server 0 percent across the board on "exceeds" and even "meets" expectations.

Bruns explains why: "We know that if the line or the wait gets too long, the customer will pass over what we call the 'cliff of dissatisfaction,' and the attitude of the employee cannot overcome that service wait. Based upon our research we know what that reasonable wait time is for every department. With these hard, unshakable facts, we can coach employees for changes in their behavior that will result in a positive change in the customer's experience." One device used to operate on the safe side of the "cliff of dissatisfaction" on a real-time basis is the Buzz Session.

Buzz Sessions. The service culture at Harrah's benefits greatly from the practice of *buzz sessions*—short department meetings at the beginning of a shift that bring the team together for five to ten minutes. Other organizations employ short, frequent meetings, but Harrah's has moved this concept to a new level. The purpose of the buzz session is to recognize that employees may have issues at home and need a transition from home to work to get ready for "showtime." The agenda for buzz sessions typically is made up of five topics—listen, communicate, reinforce, celebrate, and have fun—as shown in "Agenda for Typical Buzz Sessions at Harrah's."

Agenda for Typical Buzz Sessions at Harrah's

According to our interviews with Harrah's managers, the daily buzz session follows this agenda.

1. **Listen:** The buzz session leader, often the team's supervisor, begins the session by checking in with the team and exploring any ideas or suggestions team members might have. Leaders are accountable for acting on any employee suggestions that arise.

2. **Communicate:** This is the opportunity to share any information that might impact the team members on the floor today. For example, is Elton John not performing at the Coliseum this week? How should we respond to guests who had tickets for that show?

3. **Reinforce:** Employees actually practice one or all of the five Spotlight on Success behaviors by demonstration or role play.

4. **Celebrate:** The supervisor uses this part of the agenda to recognize employees informally or to award a service star to someone who has earned it.

5. **Have fun:** The buzz session ends with some form of fun to get the team ready to demonstrate an upbeat and positive attitude as they move onto the floor and into their roles.

Buzz sessions happen all day as shifts start and end. They often occur in front of a board displaying the property's and the department's performance on "friendly/helpful" scores and examples of positive customer comments recognizing team members. There is typically a team goal reminding everyone what the team is working on this week.

The CSA team publishes the schedule of each department's buzz sessions, and, like the Swiss railway system, they always start on time. Senior executives are expected to drop in on a number of them, and the property's general manager reviews a weekly report of who attended which meetings.

Managers must be trained and certified to run a buzz session. As Terry Byrnes, vice president for customer satisfaction assurance, explains, "Customer service directors put a lot of work into buzz sessions, because that can be the place that you build your service culture if you get them right."

Spotlight on Success. To standardize its coaching efforts, Harrah's has developed the Spotlight on Success program, a scored coaching tool that supervisors can use to rate their frontline employees' performance on each of the Spotlight 5 behaviors described earlier and provide them with targeted improvement feedback. Of special note is that the program also includes *training customers* on how to conduct a Spotlight on Success observation, complete the form, and turn it in to a third party for scoring. The two ratings—the supervisor's and the customer's—are compared by the supervisor's manager to see how aligned each was in rating a frontline service provider's performance.

Coordinating Marketing, Operations, and Human Resources at Build-A-Bear Workshop

Cross-functional coordination is critical to success at Build-A-Bear Workshop as well. Scott Gower, managing director of Workshops for the Southern United States, describes coordination between marketing and operations this way: "Marketing is critical to our concept. So our marketing and operations teams continually are looking at 'Okay, here's the idea. How are we going to execute? What is the Guest experience going to be like?'"

Operations and human resources also work together closely to deliver on the brand promise communicated by the marketing group. They are required to do this by the three elements of Build-A-Bear Workshop's operating strategy:

- Simple Excellence, an operating platform that makes it easy for frontline staff to consistently delight customers and create a memorable experience

- A service delivery system that makes memorable experiences, characterized by Wow! stories for its Guests, a routine occurrence

- The cycle of capability that underlies both of these elements

The Power of Simple Excellence. Harrah's example demonstrates the importance of keeping things simple to give frontline employees the chance to win. Build-A-Bear Workshop embraces that principle too. For example, e-mails from headquarters to each store are limited to one per week. Instructions are kept to one page. A maximum of one delivery of products is scheduled per store per week (though the company is moving to a just-in-time inventory system). And each store carries a minimum of stock with a typical store carrying less than 450 individual items with the focus on units that customers can mix and match to create maximum flexibility with mass customization.

One of our favorite examples of simple excellence is the system of delivering home-cooked meals to the business executives of Mumbai, as described in "Achieving Simple Excellence." It suggests that simple excellence doesn't require elaborate methods or sophisticated technology.

Memorable Experiences. Build-A-Bear Workshop uses cross-functional coordination to deliver the kind of memorable experiences that foster customer ownership. These experiences often result in "Wow!" stories that recognize its best Bear Builder associates as well. The heart of this effort results from the inputs of marketing, operations, and human resources to create focused employee selection, labor scheduling, and personnel development strategies.

Consider how the functions come together in the selection of marketing initiatives appropriate to the business. Build-A-Bear Workshop has, for example, partnered with organizations like the World Wildlife Fund. When a child chooses an animal from that collection, one dollar is donated to the charity. Every spring the company hosts its annual Stuffed with Hugs event, during which anyone can go to any Build-A-Bear Workshop store and stuff a bear for free; the bear is then donated to a

Achieving Simple Excellence

Many working Indians still cling to a custom of having a home-cooked meal prepared by their wives or mothers delivered to their workplace each day. The dabbawalla system for accomplishing this is the essence of simple excellence.

It begins, for example, in Mumbai, a metropolitan area of 25 million people, with the preparation of tens of thousands of meals at home that are picked up each day by 8:30 a.m. by a network of *dabbawallas* (box + the man who carries it), a group of delivery people operating on a precise schedule. Meals are carried in reusable containers with color-coded markings designating addresses, floors of buildings, and office numbers. They are taken by bicycle to the nearest commuter railroad station, where the first sort occurs. Then each dabbawalla boards a train with his *dabbas* for the ride to the neighborhood where he will deliver. At his arrival there, the boxes brought in by other dabbawallas from all over the city are once again sorted for final delivery. By 1 p.m. all deliveries are finished, allowing the dabbawallas to have lunch themselves before beginning the entire process in reverse, returning their dabbas to the homes where they were picked up originally. For this, a dabbawalla who has built up his trade can earn a substantial living, especially for a tradesman who is often illiterate.

Rarely does a dabba fail to find its destination on time, and then only when addresses become blurred on the boxes. The color-coded boxes allow even someone who cannot read to do his job flawlessly. It is a striking example of simple excellence. As one dabbawalla, Dhondu Kondaji Chowdhury, put it, "There is a service called FedEx that is similar to ours—but they don't deliver lunch."

Source: Based on Saritha Rai, "Grandma Cooks, They Deliver," *New York Times*, May 29, 2007.

charity. The charitable events not only draw crowds, but they're also some of the biggest sales days.

As President and Chief Operating Bear Scott Seay explained to us: "In today's world, when you are building a world-class lifestyle brand for families, you have to be connected in many different ways. Our retail environment and store is a big piece of that and typically starts the brand relationship. But we know it's about all kinds of family entertainment choices—like music and games and Web sites. They all build brand connectivity. Our brand will always be grounded in friendship, but our marketing and merchandise groups work hard to have partnerships and weave culturally relevant topics together with our brand."

It should be no surprise that the partnership with the World Wildlife Fund was jointly determined by marketing, operations, and human resources or that the head of operations is a particular fan of the initiative. Why? Because the promotion had to be delivered flawlessly, and it had to appeal to both young Guests and the Bear Builder associates who serve them. The initiative is not just about sales, but about building a sense of community among associates as well.

Another example of functional coordination is the labor scheduling process. Build-A-Bear Workshop has designed a very complex system that is simple to use. It takes into account factors that will determine sales per hour for each part of the day, such as previous sales volumes and trends; new promotions or activities such as parties (from its Guest Services team); whether or not a store delivery is scheduled (operations); and how many four-hour shifts will be needed (reflecting Build-A-Bear Workshop human resource reliance on part-timers). It estimates the time required at each station based on the number of skins to be stuffed and average stuffing time.

Without cross-functional cooperation, it would be impossible to predict or meet human resource needs for on-the-job training, epitomized in the "Bear Builder ladder," a simple rating system from A to D based on the level of experience and capability of each frontline associate. Once a month, the management team gets together and assesses its team members to update the ladder. Using these inputs, the labor planner ensures that a store's newest, least experienced associates are not scheduled together during a peak period; it ensures that As are working with Cs to get Cs to the next level.

Cycle of Capability. The Build-A-Bear Workshop cycle of capability is carefully crafted from selection through measurement and recognition.

The company hires only 2 to 4 percent of job applicants for store manager positions. But everyone who applies gets a response. For the associate role, the company looks first for someone who is "caring," then for
the ability to engage Guests. As a result, applicants "audition" in group
interviews of five to ten at a time. Prospects are asked questions or given
tasks to see how comfortable they are being "on stage," which is what will
be expected of them at times during their in-store experiences. Managers
then select which applicants they want to call back for in-depth interviews, designed to test for evidence of characteristics of successful current associates and managers. As Scott Gower, managing director,
Stores–East Region, puts it, "Hiring seventeen- to nineteen-year-old
people who can create that fun is a very difficult thing to do. Having fun
and making fun are two really different things."

Like other organizations in our study, the most important source of candidates is associate referrals, which account for over 30 percent of new store
management hires. Darlene Elder, managing director, Bear and Human
Resources, comments: "Some of our best referrals come from our associates. After all, would you refer somebody who wasn't going to also help you
and your company be successful? So it's a win/win situation, and we reward
our successful associate referrals with a special thank-you bonus."

Onboarding is critical, and at Build-A-Bear Workshop it encompasses
all the steps from the job application to the associate's future development
experience. After a common introduction, associates and managers
undergo separate training routes. For both, training on the job is critical.

There are service standards for each touch point in a Build-A-Bear
Workshop store. Each associate is trained in ways to meet them to ensure
that a Guest receives a consistent and yet personalized experience. For
example, a particularly emotional part of the experience comes during
the heart ceremony when the Guests select a special heart and make a
wish that will stay with their new friend forever. The heart is warmed in
their hands, kissed on both sides, and tucked inside the stuffed animal
with a special wish. It was devised by high-performing Bear Builder
associates who came up with the idea in the early years of Build-A-Bear

Workshop (a good example of the importance of employee ownership). It was inserted into the training and operations for all stores.

Bear Builder associates are moved from station to station to keep them fresh and upbeat over their four-hour shift. This requires that they be cross-trained. They are then given latitude within limits to care for Guests. When problems arise, they are encouraged to handle them immediately. Scott Gower comments, "We are focused on having a 'yes' culture. If a Guest is not completely satisfied, I want my team to focus on turning the experience into a complete wow. Find out what will make the Guest happy and do it. Just say yes. It empowers our store teams to act and take the action necessary—without seeking approval from layers in the organization—to make someone's day."

Quality of work life is central to the cycle of capability at Build-A-Bear Workshop. It includes everything from dress code to hours worked. For example, shorts or khaki pants, tennis shoes, and a denim shirt is the order of the day in stores where Bear Builder associates may spend time on the floor with Guests. World Bearquarters in St. Louis has a similar casual dress code and associates can even bring their pet dogs to work, fostering a relaxed and friendly atmosphere that the company believes increases its creativity and productivity.

Store managers work five eight-hour days a week, compromising a relatively short work week for a retail store manager. But it is important to a strategy of delivering delight through upbeat, positive experiences.

Build-A-Bear Workshop measures sales volume and mix of business every hour in every store. Guest satisfaction is measured as well, through either an interactive voice response system or a Web-based system that allows Guests to provide feedback to Build-A-Bear Workshop immediately after their store visits. Each month store managers receive their updated results and meet with their teams during preshift meetings to review the results and determine actions needed for improvement.

Recognition plays a larger role than money in the Build-A-Bear Workshop reward system for associates. Scott Gower comments, "The majority of our team members are committed to our Guests and our company.

They're not expecting anything back. They just want to be really good at their job. Sometimes, simple recognition goes far. 'Hey—you're doing a great job and I'm glad you're on the team.' We put a lot more effort into our rewards and recognition programs, but sometimes it's that heartfelt acknowledgement that makes all the difference in the world."

Nevertheless, in cooperation with marketing, the company provides incentives on what it expects to be challenging days during the big volume holiday season, which they refer to as "Wow-i-days." For example, past events have included each store receiving a stack of $5 certificates to hand out when associates go above and beyond the normal expectations. The money is then added to their next paychecks. Also, the month of September (not a peak traffic month) is "Bear Builder Appreciation Month." Every Bear Builder associate who has been with the company for ninety days gets, in addition to special gifts, a paid day off.

Finally, there is a weekly ritual of recognition that has become part of the management fabric at Build-A-Bear Workshop. Maxine Clark describes it this way:

> While we receive sales data every day from stores all over the world, every weekend we have the stores e-mail us their results directly. There's a group of us—myself, our CFO, Scott—and what we do is respond back to them like, "Great day. Your average transactions are really good." We look at the details that they give us, and we try to reinforce the positive behaviors that we want, that each store needs to be looking at in order to make their weekend come out. They love it because they have personal contact with us, and sometimes it's a game to see who responds first. If it's midnight and it's in California, it's later than that for us. So we're pretty much on it all the time, and by the time I go to bed on a Saturday night, I have responded to every single store that's open. I really enjoy it. We all do it, and it's sort of part of our tradition.

Clark likes to say, "We've got a big company mentality and a small company heart." The weekend e-mail ritual is a good example of that. It continues even though Build-A-Bear Workshop now operates over 325 company-owned stores.

DYNAMIC DELIVERY SYSTEMS AT WORK

All of the systems, policies, and practices we've discussed thus far translate into the value that's created when frontline employees interact with guests. That's where demand is matched to capacity and vice versa in the pursuit of delight. So the last big step in anticipatory management is learning to adjust capacity to demand—and demand to capacity—in real time as the need arises. Both Harrah's and Build-A-Bear Workshop have developed dynamic delivery systems to do just that.

Harrah's Entertainment: The Active Enterprise

Two or three times as many customers visit Harrah's on weekends as on weekdays. Weekend days have become known as "focus days," when Harrah's associates must be at their best. Measuring the patterns of customer behavior by type of customer and by the day of week and time of day is essential to create the full capacity to serve. But these decisions then must result in real action on the casino floor. That's where key results and dynamic delivery systems become important.

Buzz sessions, as you saw earlier, are an example of dynamic delivery systems at work on the floor of a Harrah's casino. But other methods are employed, in, for example, the coordination of demand and capacity.

Matching Demand to Capacity. Dynamic value delivery systems require cross-functional coordination. At Harrah's, engineering ownership begins with determining what is required to create a great moment of truth. This involves a hierarchy of responsibilities and actions, beginning with the senior management responsibility of matching demand to capacity, requiring coordination between marketing and operations. John

Bruns describes how difficult this coordination was: "I would say it took probably two to three years . . . to understand how to pull the triggers on dynamic delivery systems. For example, when we went after customers that we had never tackled before, we overloaded the system. We had a huge gain in gross gaming revenue. But we didn't have enough people or capacity to serve. So while the revenues and profit went sky-high, the service started to decline dramatically. We're talking a six-point drop."

Matching Capacity to Demand. Harrah's managers must adjust capacity dynamically to meet changes in demand. And they must do so seamlessly, in real time, while continuing to exceed expectations, especially those of Seven Star and Diamond customers. In some cases this means managing the physical asset of the casino itself. In others, it relies mostly on dynamic systems and processes. Nowhere is this more evident than in the management of wait lines. It is one of two key attributes, along with "friendly/helpful," that drives customer satisfaction and loyalty at Harrah's.

Waiting is a fact of life in a service business; it's the equivalent of a manufacturer's inventory. But minimizing the time customers spend waiting frees them to engage in other activities that generate value for them and for the organization. So Harrah's makes a bold promise to its Seven Star and Diamond customers: "You are always next in line." If key result customers at Harrah's are virtually never waiting, the economics can be staggering.

Harrah's management understands that three elements influence a guest's perceptions of wait time in a line.

- *Actual time in line:* This refers to the actual time the guest has been waiting to be served.

- *Number of people in line:* Harrah's has found that no matter how quickly the line moves, the number of people ahead of the guest influences a guest's perception of how long the wait is.

- *Transaction time:* The amount of time it takes to complete the service a customer is waiting for. It is less important than the other two factors, because it involves an interaction over which an employee can have some control.

Wait line management is especially important at the key results areas described earlier, where Harrah's differentiates the customer experience to surprise and delight its high-value players. Two such areas are slot dispatch and cashier (or cage) operations. Slot dispatch, described at the outset of this chapter, uses a great deal of technology. Cashier operations, on the other hand, do not. Here's how it works.

Imagine you are a Diamond player on a Saturday night wanting to cash some chips. As you approach the cashier station you see that there are ten windows available. However, only eight of them are actually open and staffed with a cashier. Of the eight open windows, five have signs that say "Seven Star and Diamond," and the other three have signs that say "All." You enter the line that is marked "Diamond." There are Diamond customers being served at each of the five Seven Star and Diamond windows, and another five Diamond players ahead of you in the line. There are eight customers in the "All" line being served by three windows.

What are associates instructed to do next? They implement a policy known as "Expedite, but don't exclude." It means that there are times when the manager decides to change the capacity of the department to ensure that the department is meeting its service standards for key result customers, but in a way that does not make its Gold customers feel excluded. The standard that is set for this cashier key result area is that with five windows open, the line for Seven Stars and Diamonds "goes red" at six players in line. So the manager of the cashier department must get the Diamond line back into standard immediately.

To do it, the manager either opens another window if a cashier is available—a costly move—or approaches the line and becomes what Harrah's calls an *expediter*. Assuming that the manager chooses the second alternative, the first thing they do will be to ensure all Diamond guests in line have a Diamond card. Non-Diamonds will be asked to move to the end of the "All" line. The expeditor will then see if they can expedite the first few

"All" customers by escorting them to one of the self-service cash machines. If the line is still not back into standard and there are no staff available to open another window, the manager will turn one of the "All" windows into a "Seven Star and Diamond" window as soon as the Gold customer at the window has been served. She then escorts the next waiting Diamond customer to the window, reducing the line length to five. She approaches the next customer in the "All" line, a customer who may be a bit upset to see that the window changed. This is when the expediter applies the "expedite but don't exclude" policy. The expediter is trained to first empathize with the customer if he or she is upset. She then sees whether there is anything she can do to expedite that Gold customer. Depending on the situation, she may even explain to the customer why the windows were changed and why that Diamond customer went ahead of him, in the process illustrating some of the benefits of consolidating their play at Harrah's. All this happens like clockwork.

Build-A-Bear Workshop: The Dynamic Learning Organization

Marketing, operations, human resources, and information systems all contribute to the dynamic delivery of Guests' experiences at Build-A-Bear Workshop. For example, shifts are typically limited to four hours, the maximum that associates are thought to be able to maintain an upbeat, spontaneous, high-intensity contribution to the company's promise of a genuine, memorable Guest experience. The floor leader, designated for each four-hour shift, is central to this. She works across the entire store, watching the flow of Guests and personally helping out to balance capacity among work stations. She is the advocate for the Guests, interacting with them to help set their expectations; the on-the-job trainer for associates throughout the shift; and also the lead sales person, ensuring that Guests know about the accessories and other items that are available for their animals.

Before each shift, floor leaders conduct a meeting with associates to discuss assignments, plans, and goals for the day for each associate. As a team they talk about such things as Guest service opportunities and new promotions. Then individual follow-up conversations during the shift provide coaching or feedback. A post-shift meeting lets the team know its results, what things it accomplished successfully, and what could have been improved. This is a learning organization at work.

As with Harrah's, lines are endemic to the process. This is a "theme park" experience in a retail setting, so standing in line comes with the territory. But that doesn't mean it is always enjoyable for the Guest. So team members have to look for ways to both delight and occupy waiting Guests. At times, this is accomplished by a floating associate helping Guests prepare for the next station, or engaging them to write their name on their "ticket" so that as they approach the Stuffing Station, for example, the associate there can know their name without asking. Other contingency plans turn waiting into fun with several "line management plays" such as "Line Lotto," "Bear Conga," or an all-time favorite of sports fans, the "Line Wave." That's why Bear Builder associates are hired in part for their ability to entertain.

The information systems help each store team make real-time operating adjustments. With the touch of one button, a chief workshop manager can see the store's average ticket (or Honey Per Guest), sales volume, and, most importantly, the store's performance on a measure called "shoes and sounds as a percentage of skins." Shoes and sounds are two of the most popular add-on categories. Consequently, "shoes and sounds as a percentage of skins" is a key metric (deep indicator), discussed in chapter 2, of the success of the business model of Build-A-Bear Workshop.

Providing feedback to the chief workshop manager on a real-time basis allows the manager to take action before the end of a shift. Like Harrah's, Build-A-Bear Workshop understands that providing information on goals and standards that are predictive allows the managers and the store team to change service or sales tactics before they have missed their goals or performance standards for a given work shift. In sum, the dynamic delivery system at Build-A-Bear Workshop makes winners of Guests and associates alike.

TECHNOLOGY ENABLES; PEOPLE DELIVER

One final point is worth noting. The science of delivering value may be enabled by superior data systems, the information developed from the data, and the way information is organized and disseminated to those who can make the best use of it. But managers at both Harrah's Entertainment and Build-A-Bear Workshop never lose sight of the reason for all this: to enable those in frontline contact with customers to win. Technology is only one element of a strategy that includes carefully creating cross-functional teams, training people in the mission of the work and simple ways of adjusting to the shifting needs of customers, granting people the latitude to do what is necessary at any moment to deliver value to customers, and giving them recognition and rewards for doing so.

ACHIEVING PROFOUND RESULTS

This detailed look at Harrah's Entertainment and Build-A-Bear Workshop describes the power of marketing, operations, and human resources working together to engineer employee and customer ownership. Tim Stanley, chief information officer at Harrah's, sums up the customer side of the strategy this way: "We want to make our interactions with customers— whether they take place on the phone, on our website, or at a slot machine—more dynamic and proactive. We're taking what we've done with our data warehouse, operational systems, and our CRM environment and integrating those initiatives in an active environment, so when someone checks into a hotel, we know exactly what needs to take place on the property to provide them with a seamless experience."[9]

Anticipatory management requires, first, the development of communities of customers, either naturally in network-based businesses or in a manufactured manner through the development of affinity programs. The data provided by these communities must be processed into information designed to enable the organization to interact with customers on an individual, customized basis. For a seamless customer experience, the data must be made available across the organization to those who are responsible for customer touch points.

This kind of data management may require reorganization. It may, for example, suggest the need for the delivery of customer experiences through teams of associates representing marketing, operations, and human resources. Where possible, the best practitioners of anticipatory management provide reasons for customers to remain in the communities that have been so carefully crafted. This practice provides a foundation for customer ownership.

Anticipatory management has had a profound impact on the performance of both Harrah's Entertainment, where enterprise value was increased three times in five years under Gary Loveman's leadership, and at Build-A-Bear Workshop, where Maxine Clark has built an organization that today employs seventy-two hundred associates and a business that has produced over $2 billion in revenue and $114 million in income in its first eleven years. But Build-A-Bear Workshop is about more than just dollars. The entire organization is designed to help teams make every Guest feel like a treasured member of the bear community. And they succeed in simple and profound ways, as illustrated in one of the many Wow! stories about unforgettable experiences for Guests and associates that we heard there. Scott Gower tells the story this way:

> This party comes into a store, and the party mom is in her
> business suit. She's got her briefcase, cell phone, and Blackberry.
> You could tell she was a control person. She gets everything
> going, and she's sitting back in the back of the store and
> conducting business while her children are having this party. My
> store manager went back, and said, "Excuse me, ma'am. Are you
> with this party?" And she was like, "Yes." And he said, "Is that
> your daughter?" And she was like, "Yes." Then he says, "Can't you
> put the phone down for a little bit? We want you to have fun too."
> He was doing it in a nice way, but she was a little ticked off at the
> beginning. But they got her involved. After they left, she came

back to the store to see him with tears in her eyes. She could only manage to get out two words to say to him: "Thank you." We have stories like that all the time.

The very best practitioners apply anticipatory management internally, too, anticipating and responding to employees' needs and concerns as carefully as they do for customers. In so doing, they build winning cultures that help sustain standards of excellence and foster ownership among customers and employees alike. We turn to the subject of culture next.

7

Build a Strong and Adaptive Ownership Culture

Why is it that many of the same companies appear repeatedly on lists of the best places to work, the best providers of customer service, and the most profitable in their industries? When we talk with leaders of these organizations, some of which have changed the rules for competing in entire industries, they point to culture as a primary reason for their success. Just as important, it's an advantage that competitors find hard to duplicate. What do managers at the best places to work understand that others don't?

For one thing, they recognize that culture is anything but the soft, mushy set of platitudes some leaders think it is. Managers in high-OQ companies understand that the identification of organization values is meaningless without a determination of the behaviors, measures, and actions that reinforce the values. They know that strong cultures can lead to success *or* to failure—and that may be another reason culture gets a bad rap in some corporate circles. But people like Al Stubblefield, CEO of Baptist Health Care (BHC), understand that strong *and adaptive* cultures can foster innovation, productivity, and a sense of ownership among employees and customers—all important elements in leveraging value over costs. This flexibility gives them a much higher probability than less adaptive organizations of producing extraordinary growth and earnings.[1]

Stubblefield knows that it's possible to develop a strong and adaptive ownership culture where one hasn't previously existed. And it doesn't take a lifetime to do so. It takes steady and persistent efforts to shape these hallmarks of culture:

- A strongly shared sense of purpose, falling just short of that of a cult

- A set of values and behaviors that embody a shared purpose

- A clear distinction between core values and customs or strategies

- Constant communication of purpose and values through senior management behavior, organization-wide performance metrics, and corrective actions when necessary

- Strong leadership that both reinforces the culture and preserves its adaptability

CHANGING THE RULES OF THE GAME THROUGH CULTURE

Remember the enthusiastic, idea-generating BHC employees we introduced in chapter 5—the ones with the "I Own Baptist Hospital" T-shirts? They didn't always feel that way. In the years leading up to 1995, BHC grew primarily through acquisition, as part of the roll up of the hospital industry. BHC leadership had spent five years in talks to bring about three major mergers that didn't materialize, creating uncertainty in the ranks of employees. It then turned its attention internally to an unsuccessful reengineering effort that was perceived as putting everyone's job at risk. A survey of employees found not only that they rated BHC below the norm on thirteen of eighteen dimensions, but also they rated the organization's leadership eight standard deviations below the norm for other organizations using the survey.

Patient satisfaction scores also fell to the eighteenth percentile rank among U.S. hospitals; that is, 82 percent of all hospitals had higher scores than BHC. Two major hospital chains with local affiliates and many more financial resources were outspending BHC. In October 1995 the board called a meeting to discuss patient satisfaction and the fact that BHC's market share was beginning to fall. As Stubblefield tells it, "If we're going to get people to drive past those other two hospitals, our simple thought was we've got to give them a reason to want to come down here. We've got to outserve these guys. We're never going to outspend them on facilities or on equipment. And you can't even outprogram them. If we're going to get people to drive down here, we've got to do it on service."[2]

So Stubblefield decided to go for broke:

> I walked into our board meeting and promised that we would raise our patient satisfaction scores from the eighteenth percentile . . . to the seventy-fifth percentile in nine months . . . When I walked out of the room after making that announcement, one of my senior officers took me aside and said, "Do you realize what you just did in there? You set us up for failure!" Nine months later, when we had not only reached the seventy-fifth percentile but surpassed it, that officer was no longer with the organization. He and a handful of others who were unwilling to completely embrace our new culture had to be replaced . . . We quickly realized that the satisfaction of our patients was directly related to the satisfaction of our employees.[3]

Stubblefield and his team set out to make BHC an outstanding place to work, primarily by codifying its culture on the kinds of values that foster ownership. In only four years—by 2000—the new culture propelled BHC to the ninety-ninth percentile in patient satisfaction, a stunning accomplishment by any measure.

For Irving Oil, a regional retailer of petroleum and convenience stores, the wake-up call came from two directions. By 2003 Irving's convenience retail (CR) business had succeeded in creating a significant footprint beyond Atlantic Canada into northern New England. But this expansion had come at a cost, and the year ended with the division missing its economic profit targets as capital charges outpaced net margin performance. The business had to turn around its financial performance. Harry Hadiaris, the general manager of the CR business, characterized the situation for us: "The business needed to produce the type of return on capital that we were being asked to achieve by our executive officer. Number one, we were not generating enough economic profit; we weren't generating the type of return required."[4]

The company was also facing a new competitive reality. With more than 250 convenience retail stores and several hundred dealers, Irving Oil was competing across a larger geography, with formidable competitors. Lou Beam, then director of operations, describes the situation: "All of a sudden we had competitors that we never imagined would be our competition. And they offered great opportunities for their and our customers. We knew that unless we did something different—and we weren't sure what that had to be—we were going to be a victim. We might not survive."

Just how Al Stubblefield, Harry Hadiaris, and others like them have fostered a culture that would transform and grow their organizations is our concern here. Most of them start by creating a shared sense of purpose.

Create a Strong Sense of Shared Purpose—but Stay Short of a Cult

Purpose is self-evident in the work some organizations do. Few would question that Baptist Health Care is in the business of saving and improving the quality of lives. Others, including Wal-Mart, Vanguard Financial Group, ING Direct, and Southwest Airlines, are on a crusade to save money for customers while delivering the highest levels of customer satisfaction. *Crusade* is not too strong a term to describe how these organizations approach their missions.

As you have seen, people must be "orange" to work at ING Direct. The color is everywhere both inside the company and in its promotional materials. It is shorthand for a fanatical pursuit of value centered on cost savings, ease of access, and high rates of return for customers. Employees are enlisted in the crusade through incentives, contests, and requests for feedback concerning the way things are done.

Similarly, employees at Vanguard Financial Group earn performance-based pay in large part by cutting costs and fees to investors. At Wal-Mart, the auditorium where management meetings are held is dominated by a large electronic sign counting up worldwide savings for customers every two seconds.

At Baptist Health Care, the quest is to provide superior service to "customers" (not patients) and to "improve the quality of life for people and communities served." To do this, hospital employees as well as physicians must exhibit behaviors that are not typical of their professions. For example, those who engage customers directly must be able to work in teams, something that is difficult for many medical practitioners, especially doctors who have been placed on a pedestal in the past. Senior management must be willing to spend time on the front lines making the rounds with employees. In short, at Baptist Health Care, quality care and phenomenal levels of customer satisfaction require fealty to unconventional practices.

In a growing number of organizations, a unifying culture is a direct result of, and an important contributor to, the practices of the service profit chain, which we describe in the introduction. Constructing such a culture begins with the creation of a working environment that will attract the most talented employees, those who can establish extended, profitable relationships with targeted customers.

At Westpac, Australia's leading bank, the service profit chain is part of the organization's DNA, according to its annual report. At the Omnicom Group, the world's largest provider of advertising, public relations, and marketing services, and at Bouygues Telecom, the fastest-growing cell phone provider in France, the service profit chain provides the rationale for much of what is done at the operating level. In these organizations, if an employee doesn't buy into the tenets and metrics of the service profit chain, it may be a career-defining choice. As a result, employees speak the same kind of shorthand that is found at Baptist Health Care. Only the words and their meanings are slightly different.

For example, at BHC, the shorthand is framed by the mission, values, vision, and what the organization calls its Five Pillars of Operational Excellence. Values are accompanied by associated behaviors. Four of the pillars—people first, then service, quality, and financial—combine to produce the fifth, growth. Everyone knows the values, behaviors, and pillars and what they stand for.

The Irving Promise became that company's version of BHC's Five Pillars in 2003. If management could execute the promise successfully, the CR business would be back on its planned financial trajectory within twelve to eighteen months. Mike Crosby, chief operating officer, describes it: "The Irving Promise is our strategy around our core competency of customer service. It is our promise to our customer. It includes everything it takes to deliver that promise to that customer across the entire business. It starts with a customer, and you work your way back through the entire organization so every individual, every business process, everything we do inside the system—everything we do must be in line to make sure we're driving that intentional, consistent, and differentiated customer experience, every day, in every store, at every occasion, three shifts a day, seven days a week, 365 days a year."

But getting to that clear, succinct definition wasn't immediately obvious. The CR leadership team committed to several weeks of executive education about and planning for the service profit chain and what it would take to effectively lead and manage the change effort, including a benchmarking visit to the Ritz-Carlton Hotels that had a profound impact on the team's view of what was possible. Crosby recalls, "We took the convenience retail team down to the Ritz-Carlton. Some people thought we were a little bit nuts. We're talking about Irving Oil—we pride ourselves on clean washrooms in gas stations—going to the Ritz-Carlton, where we have ladies and gentlemen serving ladies and gentlemen? It was a little bit of a stretch for us, but I can tell you, when that team came back from that meeting they were absolutely changed."

So it doesn't matter whether you're Irving Oil or the Ritz-Carlton. You must build a strongly shared purpose. The purpose you define doesn't have to be world changing. One of our favorite service organizations and a preferred employer in the Boston metro area is Direct Tire, a tire retailing and repair company. Its primary purpose is to deliver high value for customers, in part by providing a great place to work—one that builds employee loyalty and good relationships with customers, who in turn reinforce the cycle of success through their loyalty to Direct Tire.

How strong is too strong a sense of shared purpose? One that has everyone passing around the Kool-Aid, unable to see any risks or reasons to change. This sort of cultlike culture can produce impressive results for years, but it can become so dogmatic that it becomes a drag on the organization, rendering it incapable of supporting—or even tolerating— strategic or tactical change. One way to avoid this risk, as you'll see, is to distinguish your purpose and values from your customs and strategies.

Identify Your Core Values and Behaviors

A strong set of values encompasses the shared beliefs that contribute to an organization's success. In their early stages of development, organizations tend to embody their founders' values. For example, the culture at SAS, the software solutions developer we introduce in chapter 5, clearly reflects many of the beliefs and values of founder and CEO James Goodnight. When he founded the company in 1976, Goodnight paid little attention to certain aspects of the business model. For example, he commented, "We took the IBM licensing document and just changed the name to SAS."[5] So much for that.

Instead, he concentrated on developing an organization where he would like to work, one that concentrated on listening to customers, developing software shaped to their needs, and shipping software without bugs. By hiring software engineers who shared these beliefs, Goodnight built from the beginning an organization with strongly shared values.

People at SAS avoid meetings whenever possible. Instead, communication and learning take place within and between software development teams working on practical solutions for clients. This practice has required that SAS hire only the best software engineers, those most interested in solving problems for customers. And even though software engineers typically move readily from one organization to another, SAS encourages them to commit to careers with SAS. For example, it offers one of the most extensive packages of benefits anywhere, including heavily subsidized day care, extensive health care for employees and their families, and outstanding fitness facilities, all on the company's campus.

By reducing employee turnover, these practices foster and enhance long-term customer relationships, something that in turn reinforces employees' reasons to stay. And they do stay. In spite of compensation levels on par with the North Carolina market, SAS has perhaps the highest rate of employee loyalty (with never more than 5 percent leaving in any one year) of any company in the industry.

In contrast, founders' values had little to do with the turnaround at Baptist Health Care. Instead, Al Stubblefield engaged the entire organization in establishing a new set of values and behavior. The process began with a two-day meeting for the senior management team, who then spent four months enlisting everyone else to discuss the following three questions:

- Why do we exist? (What is our mission?)

- What are we striving to become? (What is our vision?)

- What guides our everyday behavior? (What are our values?)[6]

The discussions took place among focus groups throughout the organization, with senior management involvement at several levels.

During these meetings, leaders also posed the question, "What makes a great culture?" The employee responses helped outline critical core behaviors: open communication of such things as performance feedback and ideas for doing things better, a "no secrets" environment in which the bad news is shared along with the good, and a "no excuses" environment in which employees are accountable for actions and results. The organization-wide outcome appears in "The Baptist Health Care Vision, Values, and Five Pillars of Operational Excellence."

Employee selection, self-selection, and referrals all reinforce core values in an ownership culture. BHC has created profiles for prospective employees by observing the people who are most successful in each major job category. These profiles translate into lists of questions that help screen job candidates for the traits most relevant to each position. Most are behavior based and not skill based, even in a hospital setting (remember that high-OQ companies hire for attitude, orient for values, and train for skills). Candidates interview with the members of the work teams they may join, a process called *peer interviewing*. The interviewers undergo two hours of training in questioning and listening skills.

At Irving Oil, hiring and keeping the right people begin with the values embodied in the Irving Promise. Cate Rafferty, convenience retail's head of human resources, describes how the promise helps frame the company's values for potential employees: "When we interview frontline candidates, we talk to them about an opportunity for our frontline people to be the difference. We talk to them about the fact that every single convenience store sells gas and every single store has exactly the same offer, but the difference at our stores are the people who work in our stores. It's the quality of the experience they bring to our customers, making them feel special for being in our stores, and providing them a 'wow' experience."

The opportunity to be the difference becomes a core value for employees, and it's reinforced by a variable-pay plan that's unique—if not to the industry, then certainly to the area. A quarterly review process translates each store's results—a combination of customer and financial metrics—into money in the pockets of the frontline team. So in addition to market-level hourly pay, they are rewarded for their ability to be the difference as a team.

Personal development is another core value for Irving employees. People get regular performance reviews and the opportunity to apply for every job opening in the company. The company posts all openings and strives to hire from within. Managers also work hard to encourage referrals

The Baptist Health Care Vision, Values, and Five Pillars of Operational Excellence

Our Vision: The vision of Baptist Health Care is to be the best health system in America.

Our Values: Integrity: Maintaining the highest standards of behavior. Encompasses honesty, ethics, and doing the right things for the right reasons.

Vision: The ability and willingness to look forward to the future and make decisions necessary to accomplish important goals.

Innovation: Capable of extraordinary creativity and willing to explore new approaches to improving the quality of life for all persons.

Superior Service: Committed to providing excellent service and compassionate care.

Stewardship: Dedicated to responsible stewardship of Baptist Health Care's assets and financial resources, and to community service.

Teamwork: An abiding respect for others, and a sustaining commitment to work together.

from high-performing employees. So people who are looking for a career—or who didn't necessarily know they were looking for a career—find that they can not only succeed but also move up in the organization.

With more than ten thousand employees, SAS still places primary emphasis on hiring people who share its core values and behaviors. As head of human resources Jeff Chambers puts it, this requires communicating to prospective employees that "this place is not for everybody."

Don't Confuse Values with Customs or Strategies

Strong values are not changed easily or lightly, especially when they contribute to an organization's success. Customs and strategies, on the other

THE FIVE PILLARS

Pillar	Pillar Description
People:	BHC should be employer of choice in the market area and a health care industry leader in values-based recruitment, employee satisfaction, employee retention and leadership development.
Service:	BHC must provide compassionate care and service to all customers at a level which continues to set the highest standards in the health care industry.
Quality:	BHC must achieve health care industry leading results in clinical performance.
Financial:	BHC must optimize financial results while meeting its mission to provide services to all, regardless of ability to pay, and to improve the health status and quality of life for residents of communities served.
Growth:	BHC must achieve fiscally responsible growth in volume and service locations while achieving financial targets.

Source: Baptist Health Care, internal document.

hand, need to evolve to reflect changes in the business or its competitive environment.

Employees often confuse values with customs. At Hewlett-Packard, for example, employees objected to the discontinuance of an annual companywide picnic. John Young, CEO at the time, recognized that the company had outgrown the picnic. Instead, it had to be replaced with other ways of bringing together people from various parts of the company. Picnics were not a shared value. The sense of community was.

SAS management now faces a similar issue. Given the company's strong employee retention rate, with annual turnover averaging less than 4 percent, the average age of its workforce is increasing. As a result, there is less need for day care and more need for attention to health care and retirement plans. So SAS will have to make changes in its famed benefits program to reflect the needs of most of its employees. The need for this action does not reflect a change in core values, but management will need to make sure that the employees understand that specific benefits are not shared values; caring for employees is.

Johnson & Johnson has long been known for its strategy of decentralization, which places profit responsibility on the shoulders of more than two hundred heads of operating units. When the organization's credo (a statement of its values) was put up for review and reaffirmation under CEO Jim Burke, many of its leaders questioned whether decentralization should be included. Upon reflection, they concluded that they were confusing a strategy, which could be altered to meet changing needs, with values having a more enduring quality.

Communicate, Communicate, Communicate

This practice does not mean meet, meet, meet. In lieu of meetings, SAS fosters an environment in which managers and employees communicate constantly—not downward or upward, but in all directions. It takes place in the relatively open work space. It consists of constant messages from top management concerning such things as new business, customer problems to be solved, and competitive challenges. It is part of the extensive educational programs offered by the company. And it extends to the thousands of pounds of M&M'S that are supplied to various informal gathering places throughout the company to encourage the kind of informal water cooler communication so important to problem solving. It's here that questions and messages concerning everything from new practices to recommendations for improving the organization, its work, and its results are formulated and communicated in all directions.

Communication is constant and multifaceted at Baptist Health Care, too. Both good and bad news regarding organization performance is posted in the cafeteria regularly. Employee forums, at which letters from customers are often read, are videotaped for distribution and later viewing. And the company's intranet is heavily used.

Communication can take unusual forms. For example, BHC "borrowed" what is known as the Daily Line Up from the Ritz-Carlton, where employees participate in a daily lineup at the start of their shifts. During each lineup, managers present one new service initiative or behavior, entertain suggestions, and recognize any employees who have demonstrated outstanding performance. BHC Daily works in the same way: every job team convenes for a few minutes a day to share a concept and suggest a training idea.

In BHC's Listening and Learning program, managers lead discussions on subjects such as survey results and solicit ideas for ways to improve customer service. The resulting "customer snapshot reports" compile all the employees' observations and ideas for general distribution.

At Irving Oil, there is a sharp focus on training and communication. Like all service profit chain leaders, Irving invests far more in training than called for in the ASTD (American Society for Training and Development) best-in-class benchmarks. Store trainers spend the equivalent of about three days with all new hires, orienting them to the job, the company, and individual tasks. There is also a specific Irving Promise orientation and an introduction to the company's performance management system, with a one-page planner that outlines how the employee's performance will be evaluated. Within ninety days, new employees receive feedback on how they are performing on the job, how they are managing as part of the team, how they are doing on the job functions, and how well they are delivering on the Irving Promise.

Not surprisingly, Harrah's Entertainment, whose anticipatory management capabilities are discussed in chapter 6, has used those abilities to take communication to a new level, as described in "Raising the Standard for Communication: 'Entertain Your Best' at Harrah's."

Raising the Standard for Communication: "Entertain Your Best" at Harrah's

In 2006, Harrah's launched an employee engagement initiative called Entertain Your Best. The program's objectives are to deepen the relationship between Harrah's and *each* employee by providing more than a place to work, creating an environment where people feel better because of their association with Harrah's, and building a competitive advantage and delivering excellent results.

The program's three guiding principles—get me, guide me, and root for me—challenge each manager to concentrate on interacting effectively with every employee every day. Employees rate managers on the following behaviors:

- Get me:
  - Take the time to know me.
  - Respect and understand my strengths and opportunities.
  - Be aware of my challenges.
  - Understand how to motivate me.

- Guide me:
  - Show me what success looks like.
  - Provide me with coaching, tools, and resources for success.
  - Make the path forward clear and well lit.
  - Protect me along the way.

- Root for me:
  - Be my biggest fan.
  - Celebrate my success.
  - Challenge me to do better than I ever thought I could be.
  - Create an environment where I can succeed.
  - Commit yourself to my development.

Source: Harrah's Entertainment, unpublished internal document.

Insist on the Right Leadership Behaviors

In his study of companies that have gone from good to great, Jim Collins found no pattern of charismatic behavior among their leaders. But he did find a common set of behaviors that he described as "Level 5 Leadership." He characterized level 5 leaders as those who build enduring greatness through "a paradoxical blend of personal humility and professional will."[7]

Cultures take shape with or without leadership. But rarely does a competitively superior culture emerge without it. Effective leaders set the tone for an organization through their own behaviors. For example, at Baptist Health Care, people at all levels are encouraged to engage in several "Baptist behaviors" that are peculiar to the organization—and sometimes startling to customers—but have a functional purpose. One of these is the custom of picking up trash (something Bill Marriott also does at his company's hotel properties). Then there is the "Baptist shuffle," in which people making rounds scrape their rubber-heeled shoes to erase scuff marks from polished floors. Another is walking people in need of direction to their destinations. Everyone, starting with Al Stubblefield, does these things all the time, in part because they foster a sense of being part of a culture that is something special.

Good leaders reinforce culture by demonstrating accountability for behaviors and results and fostering the same attitude among employees. At Baptist Health Care, this begins with "Traditions," a two-day orientation; half the time is focused on BHC's culture. This session is followed by "ServU," a half-day refresher course for employees who are completing six months of service and have had a chance to observe and work in the culture.

ServU focuses almost exclusively on the way employees understand and experience the BHC culture. In particular, the discussion covers the standards of performance for ten specific behaviors: attitude, appearance, communication, call lights (which all hospital employees are responsible for answering), commitment to coworkers, customer waiting, elevator etiquette, privacy, safety awareness, and sense of ownership. The BHC employee standards team also devises ways of celebrating the "standard of the month" on a rotating basis. After all this, it's hard for new employees not to understand the behaviors of choice at Baptist Health Care.

The BHC story shows clearly how a strong culture creates the potential for high performance. We say "potential," because some of our other research has suggested that strong cultures, by themselves, are not enough to drive long-term success. Leaders who foster a strong ownership culture must also preserve its ability to adapt to a changing environment. They do it by emphasizing practices that help the organization and its people grow: continuous improvement, innovation in products and services as well as management systems, education for personal development, and—again—communication, communication, communication.

AVOIDING COMMON PITFALLS

Strong cultures are not fragile. But they can be damaged by such things as management behaviors that don't reflect organization values or poorly thought-out reductions in force. Again, leadership is critical. When Lou Gerstner assumed the leadership of IBM and was asked what the company's strategy would be, he replied that he didn't know. But what he did know was that the company's values had to be reinforced. His immediate predecessors on the job had neglected them. They had failed to reinforce a knowledge of the values and desired behaviors.

In addition to failures in leadership, some of the greatest threats to a winning culture include runaway success, a loss of curiosity and interest in change, a triumph of culture over performance, a failure to reinforce desired behaviors, a breakdown in consistent communication, and leaders who are overcome by a sense of their own importance. Again, what goes on at Baptist Health Care and Irving Oil is instructive in suggesting how to combat these challenges.

The Perils of Success

Runaway success may be the greatest threat to a winning culture. One need only look at Starbucks and JetBlue, two organizations that have been lauded both for their astounding growth and for their strong cultures. Howard Schultz, chairman and CEO of Starbucks, recently announced two potentially inconsistent initiatives in the same week.

- Starbucks stores, noted for their coffee, ambience, and service-oriented staff members, needed to reestablish their individuality and relationship with the communities they serve while improving actual service levels (in the face of an expanding menu).

- Starbucks would more than double the number of stores, to a total of forty thousand in the next five years.

At JetBlue, the fastest-growing major airline in the United States at the time, the company's service was severely compromised by a February 2007 ice storm that not only forced a number of flight cancellations but also left some passengers sitting in planes for more than six hours. Worse, management lost track of its scattered crews; it was forced to phone them to find out where they were. The event was only a symptom of a deeper need for improved support systems and a better cycle of capability. Not long afterward, the JetBlue CEO agreed with the board that he should step aside. This kind of wake-up call can challenge a winning ownership culture, particularly when the cycle of capability fails and employees are unable to win in the eyes of the customer. But it also provides an opportunity to rethink what is really important to the long-term success of the organization.

Building and maintaining a winning culture take work and constant vigilance. By the time we caught up with Al Stubblefield in late 2006, the organization's dilemma reflected the success of previous years. Baptist Health Care's customer satisfaction scores had fallen back to the ninety-eighth percentile. Everyone knew about it, because the practice of sharing good and bad news involved, among other things, posting scores in the company cafeteria. As Stubblefield put it, "When we dropped to ninety-eight after seven years at ninety-nine, [the employees] panicked. They had a 'back to basics' course—put every employee in the organization through it. Because we fell to the ninety-eighth percentile." Notice that it was the employee owners who panicked and got to work to reinforce the culture at BHC.

In any change effort as comprehensive and challenging as the one faced by the CR team at Irving Oil, there are going to be mistakes—some bigger than others. And when mistakes happen, the values of the organization need to act as your compass. Cate Rafferty describes just such a situation:

> When I think about the company values, I think about how they have guided us in tough times. For example, we messed up the fourth-quarter variable pay. We determined some people had been underpaid, and some people had been overpaid. Senior people on the team got together to talk about it and asked, "What is the right thing to do here?" First thing, we needed to make whole anybody who wasn't paid correctly. The next thing was how to deal with the people that were overpaid.
>
> Since we made the mistake, at first we felt that they should keep the money. But as we dug a little deeper and compared that to our values, we realized that didn't fit our values, because it was random. If everybody got an extra twenty dollars, you could live with it. But if one person got an extra thousand dollars, and another got an extra twenty dollars, and a third didn't get anything, and she was the best performer out of the three of you—well, it just wasn't right.
>
> So the harder decision, but one that matched our culture and values, was to go to you and say, "We made a mistake. We gave you a thousand dollars that you weren't entitled to, and we are going to take that back." It was excruciating, but it was the right thing to do.

So part of living our values was that our senior managers went to every single site and met with the people, and told them it was really uncomfortable, and it was really unfortunate. "We know it stinks. Here's how it happened, and here's how we'll tell you it won't happen again, but you weren't entitled to this." And in 80 percent of the cases, it was fine.

Here is the value statement that guided this difficult decision at Irving Oil: "We believe in demonstrating commitment, keeping our word, respecting people as individuals, and providing the best for our customers."

The Loss of Curiosity and Interest in Change

An early study of companies with strong cultures and poor performance identified an important characteristic they shared. They had lost an interest in change.[8] A "not invented here" mentality had been allowed to flourish. At Texaco, for example, executives were discouraged from belonging to industry associations where ideas might be exchanged. If someone wanted to visit another company to discuss best practice, the typical response was, "Okay, but don't bring any of that back here."

Perhaps this is why Baptist Health Care engages in a continuous quality improvement effort that, as mentioned earlier, ultimately contributed to Baptist Hospital Inc. (BHI), a subsidiary of BHC, winning the Malcolm Baldrige National Quality Award in 2003—only the second hospital to receive that coveted honor. The efforts leading up to the award, including benchmarking against other organizations and continuing best-practice reviews both inside and outside BHC, have sent the message that change and innovation are important. The Bright Ideas initiative described in chapter 5 reinforces the message as it continuously engages the entire organization in suggesting process and service improvements.

The Triumph of Culture over Performance

Strong cultures are important. But they are not sufficient. In fact, they can lead to what we think of as a triumph of culture over performance.

The remedy is to make sure that your culture reinforces performance and that positive performance reinforces your culture. Few would doubt the strength of cultures at Baptist Health Care and SAS. But these organizations also are serious bottom-line performers. They track and reward behaviors as well as results, including financial performance and growth. BHC places the emphasis on behaviors. But it also identifies financial success and growth as cause for celebration.

The Failure to Reinforce Desired Behaviors

Leaders get sloppy. They fail to measure management behaviors. They postpone difficult conversations about employees who do not live the values of the organization. They delay decisions to replace such employees, especially if they are meeting their numbers.

The most successful way to combat this problem is to delegate the reinforcement of behaviors to peers, a practice that encourages every member of every work team to behave like an owner. This is what Baptist Health Care has done. Not only do teams hire new team members, but they also ensure newcomers' success through coaching and frank feedback. And they are not reluctant to replace team members who don't measure up.

The Breakdown of Consistent Communication

A culture thrives on clear, consistent communication. Unfortunately, senior managers often send conflicting messages about values and standards of behavior. Complexity is the villain in organizations that identify too many values and desired behaviors. But often, complexity and mixed messages really mean that the organization's leaders don't believe in the competitive value of "that culture stuff."

This is not the case at Baptist Health Care. Among other things, senior executives try to touch on the organization's five core values in every formal presentation to employees. The standards team designs games, contests, and activities intended to highlight one of the ten standards of behavior each month.

Leaders Overcome by a Sense of Their Importance

Leadership can go to one's head. When this happens, leaders exhibit behaviors such as talking when they should be listening, reversing the concept of servant leadership, taking too much credit for success and too little blame for failure, rewarding those who make their numbers no matter whether they manage by the values, and allowing a cult of personality to become too strong in the organization.

Strong ownership cultures avoid these foibles by constantly placing recognition where it belongs: on any employee contribution that enables the people on the front line to deliver value for customers.

The leaders we've studied find a variety of behaviors to help ensure that they are not overcome by a sense of their own importance. Sometimes this involves self-deprecating humor. Al Stubblefield, taking a cue from Southwest Airlines cofounder Herb Kelleher and CEO Gary Kelly, often finds ways of dressing up in funny costumes to illustrate some aspect of what he wants to say in a meeting with employees.

WHAT DIFFERENCE DOES CULTURE MAKE?

It's hard to measure the extent to which culture accounts for success. But as leaders like Al Stubblefield, James Goodnight, and Mike Crosby have learned, an organization that develops a strong and adaptive culture will enjoy greater loyalty from customers and employees alike.

Cultures that foster ownership create labor cost advantages because they often become better places to work, so they become well known among prospective employees. Compared with less effective cultures, they generate higher referral rates and more improvement ideas from existing employees. When this happens, the pool of prospective employees grows, and hiring costs go down as existing and prospective employees sort themselves into and out of consideration for jobs, and employee owners spend their careers helping to perpetuate the cycle of capability.

One consultant to Baptist Health Care observed that he has never seen an organization make so much progress in employee and patient satisfaction in eighteen months. And twenty-four months after Stubble-field's promise to his board, BHC's satisfaction scores surpassed any-thing the consultant had ever seen in any organization. One BHC subsidiary has received the highest customer satisfaction scores of any hospital in the United States for the past six years. At the same time, its market share has increased by five percentage points. It goes to show that there's nothing "soft" about culture in a competitive environment.

Can the advantages of culture outlast a charismatic leader? Our answer should be clear by now. But if we have fielded the question, "How will Southwest Airlines survive without Herb Kelleher?" once, we've fielded it a hundred times. Given the strong and adaptive culture South-west has developed under Kelleher's leadership and reinforced under people like President Colleen Barrett and current CEO Gary Kelly, we always respond, "Just fine as long as the culture is maintained."

BUILDING AN OWNERSHIP CULTURE: THE TOP TEN LESSONS FROM THE BEST PRACTITIONERS

We can learn a great deal from organizations whose strong and adaptive ownership cultures give them a powerful competitive edge. Here are our top ten lessons.

1. Leadership is critical in codifying and maintaining an organization's purpose, values, and vision. Leaders must set the example by living the elements of culture: values, behaviors, measures, and actions. Values are meaningless without the other elements.

2. Like anything worthwhile, culture is something in which you invest. An organization's norms and values aren't formed through speeches but through actions and team learning. Strong cultures have teeth. They are much more than slogans and empty promises. Some organizations choose to part ways with those who do not manage according to the values and behaviors that other

employees embrace. Others accomplish the same objective more positively. At Baptist Health Care, for example, managers constantly reinforce the culture by recognizing those whose actions exemplify its values, its behaviors, and its standards. Team successes are cause for frequent celebrations. In addition, BHC rewards individual accomplishments through such things as "WOW (Workers becoming Owners and Winners) Super Service Certificates," appreciation cards for ninety-day employees that list their contributions to their team, one-year appreciation awards, multiyear service awards, employee of the month awards, and recognition of workers as "Champions" or "Legends" for extraordinary achievements or service. Managers at all levels offer frequent informal recognition and send handwritten thank-you notes (which stand out in the age of e-mail). Those who aren't living up to BHC's values soon get the point.

3. Employees at all levels in an organization notice and validate the elements of culture. As owners, they judge every management decision to hire, reward, promote, and fire colleagues. Their reactions often come through in comments about subjects such as the "fairness of my boss." The underlying theme in such conversations, though, is the strength and appropriateness of the organization's culture.

4. Organizations with clearly codified cultures enjoy labor cost advantages for the following reasons:

   – They often become better places to work.

   – They become well known among prospective employees.

   – The level of ownership—referral rates and ideas for improving the business from existing employees—is often high.

   – The screening process is simplified, because employees tend to refer acquaintances who behave like them.

– The pool of prospective employees grows.

– The cost of selecting among many applicants is offset by cost savings as prospective employees sort themselves into and out of consideration for jobs.

– This self-selection process reduces the number of mismatches among new hires.

5. Organizations with clearly codified and enforced cultures enjoy great employee and customer loyalty, in large part because they are effective in either altering ineffective behaviors or disengaging from values-challenged employees in a timely manner.

6. An operating strategy based on a strong, effective culture is selective of prospective customers. It also requires the periodic "firing" of customers, as pointed out in our examples of companies like ING Direct, where thousands are fired every month. This strategy is especially important when customers "abuse" employees or make unreasonable demands on them.

7. The result of all this is "the best serving the best," or as Ritz-Carlton's mission states, "Ladies and gentlemen serving ladies and gentlemen."

8. This self-reinforcing source of operating leverage must be managed carefully to make sure that it does not result in the development of dogmatic cults with little capacity for change. High-performing organizations periodically revisit and reaffirm their core values and associated behaviors. Further, they often subscribe to some kind of initiative that requires constant benchmarking and searching for best practices both inside and outside the organization. For example, at Baptist Health Care, all employees are expected and encouraged "to search until they find 'the best of the best' in their area of expertise and benchmark against them (and possibly emulate them)."[9]

9. Organizations with strong and adaptive cultures foster effective succession in the leadership ranks. In large part, the culture both prepares successors and eases the transition.

10. Cultures can sour. Among the reasons for this are success itself, the loss of curiosity and interest in change, the triumph of culture over performance, the failure of leaders to reinforce desired behaviors, the breakdown of consistent communication, and leaders who are overcome by their own sense of importance.

We have learned repeatedly that there is a pattern in the actions and activities involved in developing strong and adaptive ownership cultures. When an organization consistently builds and reinforces such a culture, it creates a competitive edge that is hard to replicate.

Challenges like the one the employee owners at Baptist Health Care faced in slipping from the ninety-ninth to the ninety-eighth percentile in customer satisfaction are the kinds of problems that most organizations would like to have. A strong and adaptive ownership culture not only responds more effectively to adversity and opportunities but also helps lock in success. Chapter 8 examines how high-OQ organizations maintain a sustainable competitive edge.

Sustain Your Success

Remember the granddaddy of all best-seller management books, *In Search of Excellence*?[1] One criticism of the book was that many of the organizations it cited fell from the ranks of the excellent after its publication. However fair the criticism, it underscores the difficulty of locking in success. All the companies in our study work hard to overcome that challenge: they never stop innovating and improving the processes that sustain employee and customer ownership. Their unflagging efforts point the way to a new era in leadership and management. And even though there's no guarantee that they won't occasionally run into trouble just as other exemplary organizations have, the relentless focus on ownership improves their odds of sustaining success.

Gary Hamel identifies Google as a leading practitioner of what he calls the future of management.[2] Google has all the indicators of a high-OQ organization. The company hires only the brightest employees who subscribe enthusiastically to the vision of helping people all over the world access the information they need. New hires find their way without many guidelines: there are no internal titles, and only broadly defined assignments, for small self-formed and self-managed teams.

The company allots 20 percent of employees' time on the job to use as they see fit—no questions asked. Most Googlers use that time to develop interests and ideas outside Google's core businesses. If they can sell their ideas within the organization, get colleagues to beta test their prototypes, and demonstrate potential, they can access management support to fund formal efforts. It's a self-managed process. With fifty to one hundred direct reports, it would be difficult for any manager to keep track of all the ideas whizzing around. No one checks to see whether people are using their free time usefully. But everyone knows that a winning project or idea can earn handsome rewards. Founders Awards, given to recognize innovative effort, can range as high as several million dollars' worth of restricted Google stock.

Google's approach generates a constant stream of new ideas among employees, who can easily find and join teams working on projects that pique their interest. A recent study found that information moved fastest among Googlers who sat closest to one another on their jobs, an endorsement of the company's "third rule for managing knowledge workers: Pack them in."[3] This unremarkable finding accompanied a more striking one: that employees move offices about every ninety days. One of the study's authors reported that employees move so often that they don't unpack.[4]

A clear-cut chain of command would be difficult to maintain in this relatively unstructured (but carefully designed) innovation machine. Instead, the organization relies almost entirely on its high employee OQ. "Life and Work at a High-OQ Organization: How Google Describes Its Jobs for Prospective Candidates," culled from the Google Jobs Web pages, offers as concise and clear a depiction of a high-OQ organization as any we've seen.

Two support systems are particularly helpful in Google's idea-generating culture. One is an intranet location where every project under development has its own Web site, accessible to everyone else in the organization. Team members are motivated to keep their Web sites current, because it encourages an exchange of ideas with those from other teams as well as cooperation among teams that might otherwise be unaware of similar interests.

Life and Work at a High-OQ Organization: How Google Describes Its Jobs for Prospective Candidates

At Google, our strategy is simple: we hire great people and encourage them to make their dreams a reality.

LIFE AT GOOGLE

Google is not a conventional company, and we don't intend to become one. True, we share attributes with the world's most successful organizations—a focus on innovation and smart business practices comes to mind—but even as we continue to grow, we're committed to retaining a small-company feel. At Google, we know that every employee has something important to say, and that every employee is integral to our success. And where else can a newbie unabashedly and unflinchingly skate over a corporate officer during a roller hockey game?

Google has offices around the globe, from Bangalore to Zurich, but regardless of where we are, we nurture an invigorating, positive environment by hiring talented, local people who share our commitment to creating search perfection and want to have a great time doing it. Googlers thrive in small, focused teams and high-energy environments, believe in the ability of technology to change the world, and are as passionate about their lives as they are about their work.

We're always on the look-out for new Googlers.

LET'S WORK TOGETHER

Chances are you have a good idea of where you want to go in life. At Google, we've designed a culture that helps you get there. From our flexible, project-based approach to corporate structure to our innovative perks and benefits, we do everything we can to make sure our employees not only have great jobs, but great lives. Into being challenged? Into having fun? Want to change the world? If the answer is yes, then you've come to the right place.

Source: Excerpted from Google jobs site, Google Inc. Used with permission. April 8, 2008.

The other support system is Google Labs, which posts potential Google offerings and invites users outside the company to beta test the offerings and share feedback and suggestions for improving them. Although it's common throughout the dot-com world to put customers to work this way, the practice has the added effect of enhancing Google's customer OQ.

What kinds of results have these practices produced? How about the fact that roughly half of recent new product launches have resulted from projects elected by employees? Or that Google was named the best place to work in the United States in 2007?[5] Or that, even though Google has now reached a substantial size, the company's profits continue to increase at a rapid pace?

This convergence of remarkable accomplishments is more than a coincidence. And much of it is the result of the ownership phenomenon.

COUNTERING THE CRITICS

Invariably when we discuss such success stories with others, someone will say something like, "Just wait until bureaucracy seeps into Google, along with growth and size." Or they'll say that what applies to an Internet-based company—for example, the concept of the beta test and customer engagement in product development—just won't work elsewhere.

Sometimes they cite the rise and fall of People Express, an airline founded in the 1980s on the principles of an equity stake for all employees, a complete absence of hierarchy, and a culture of self-sufficiency. (One of our colleagues recalls a board meeting in which the chief financial officer had to excuse himself to run off copies of some materials the board needed, while the directors waited.) Such unusual management practices were not the only reason for the company's ultimate failure. In fact, many observers marveled at its spectacular early success. But when People Express collapsed under a mountain of debt following a string of acquisitions that it had trouble integrating and from a disastrous shift in market focus, the debacle gave employee ownership a bad name—especially, some said, for organizations larger than a certain size.

Despite the wary comments about Google's management philosophy and the scary recollections of People Express, the concept of ownership is not a fragile one, especially if it is thoughtfully practiced and ingrained in the culture of an organization.

You may have noted that many of the examples we've turned up in our research represent midsized organizations. These may be where the incubators of ownership are found today. We don't believe for a moment that ideas spawned in companies like ING Direct, Wegmans, and Baptist Health Care can't be applied in the largest of organizations. But it requires constant attention.

It may seem somehow easier to build an organization that fosters ownership when you're starting from scratch, as you've seen at Google, Build-A-Bear Workshop, and SAS. However, even as a founder you'll need to get all the ingredients right for your company, and make sure they remain relevant over time.

In existing organizations such as Baptist Health Care, the New York Police Department, Irving Oil, and Harrah's Entertainment, the task of building ownership poses a much larger challenge. Some skeptics question whether it can be done at all—whether any combination of initiatives can recast organizations more than twenty or so years old to respond to the expectations and challenges of the future. Our response? If a company adopts an ownership state of mind—which begins with a redefined strategic value vision and proceeds through the rest of the steps we've described in this book—of course it can.

BUILDING AN OWNERSHIP STATE OF MIND

Leading and *managing* are terms somewhat antithetical to the world of ownership. Owners, especially customers, don't like to be led and managed. Any effort to lead or manage owners can be likened to herding cats.

Instead, managers in a world of ownership must set out the equivalent of cat food in order to induce any kind of organized behavior.

Ownership must be fostered, encouraged, and nourished in all the ways we've described. It requires measuring the things that matter, yes, but also intense listening and intelligent responses to the issues your measures reveal. It requires engaging continuously in focused conversations to produce individualized outcomes for customers or employees. And it requires deciding just how much customer and employee ownership produces the desired financial results—the ultimate test of ownership.

Most important, it requires what we call an ownership state of mind, which starts with a strategic value vision, a careful choice of customers as well as employees, and an operating strategy and culture that can deliver what both groups value most. The ownership state of mind helps employees—and also customers—work together in cross-functional teams, with outstanding support systems and continuous communication that fuel a never-ending quest for improvement in value for employees and customers. And it requires leaders who are confident enough to set the example and thrive in such an environment.

Define a Value-Driven Strategy

The strategic value vision should not only inspire but also allow employees to envision the results they seek, even if the goals are ambitious. Consider Google's lofty vision of organizing and making accessible the world's information for every individual user.

Even the most seemingly mundane business can have an inspiring value vision. One of our favorite examples is Mexico-based Cemex, the world's third-largest producer of cement and related products. Cemex never would have achieved global prominence if its leader, Lorenzo Zambrano, had seen it as a cement company. Instead, Zambrano regularly reminds his management team, "Who wants a sack of cement? You want a home or a bridge or a runway."[6] On another occasion, Zambrano expanded the concept: "In the end, we're selling timeliness and quality and the image of a company that is at the top of its class."[7]

This strategic value vision opens a range of business opportunities that transcends cement for Cemex. Managers from more than fifty countries place their suggestions for new business opportunities in an "idea bank," which is managed centrally by the company's Innovation Committee. The bank helps managers share and refine these suggestions as they implement hundreds of ideas worldwide every year.

All this takes place in an organization that has hired carefully, trained well, and provided outstanding worldwide support systems that enable managers to focus on entrepreneurial activities rather than routine administrative chores. The standardized, centrally managed systems help integrate newly acquired companies into Cemex's network and maximize flexibility: managers can travel or move from one part of the world to another and be up to speed on the support systems and networks within fifteen minutes after arrival. The company calls this overall approach "The Cemex Way." It's a significant psychological distance from the image that most of us have of the cement industry.

Hire for Excellence

Neither Google nor Cemex would be able to foster high-speed innovation if they didn't hire the very best people for their respective organizations. The ownership quotient lives or dies by the quality of initial employee selection. So, like it or not, hiring becomes the single most important responsibility for leaders in such companies. And because relationships are crucial to ownership, new hires must be able to work in teams.

Encourage Teamwork

Not all organizational challenges yield to a team approach. But smoothly functioning teams have a natural tendency to foster ownership. If teams are structured properly, their members can depend on one another. They often share responsibility for shepherding an idea or dealing with a customer problem from beginning to end.

In the process, they develop a strong sense of commitment to their teams and to the organization. This dedication is reflected in their tendency to monitor the quality of their own work, contribute ideas for process and product improvement, and recommend friends as potential team members.

Create Cross-Functional Coordination at All Levels

Organizations with high ownership quotients seek opportunities to create cross-functional coordination. Sometimes it takes place in cross-functional teams, but coordination may take other forms. For example, when slow growth or sluggish markets caused a severe imbalance in supply and demand for steelmaker Nucor several years ago, management took the opportunity to send manufacturing people into the field to assist with sales and refill the order pipeline.

Exchange Information Openly with Employees and Customers

Open exchange is a way of life at Google. In the short term, this kind of openness may not always work to the company's competitive advantage—for example, when communities of employees and customers leak information to competitors or others. But the long-term benefits of open exchange, particularly in the improvement of products and services, more often outweigh the risks. This is particularly true in the information economy, which is making it increasingly difficult to hoard information and ideas or maintain confidentiality.

Combine Listening and Acting

If ownership is to flourish, those who listen must have the latitude to act. An organization's ability to respond to employee or customer proposals and suggestions (as well as problems) is compromised with every handoff that takes place between those who listen and those who act. In the most successful cases we've observed, the responsibilities converge.

ADDRESSING THE LEADERSHIP ISSUES

Organizations that foster ownership pose unique issues for leaders. In particular, leaders need to address three important questions: first, whether managers and employees at all levels have sufficient self-confidence to foster an ownership culture; second, how much and what kinds of ownership are needed; and third, whether appropriate methods for measurement, recognition, and rewards are in place.

Do Your Managers Have the Self-Confidence to Practice "Non-Zero-Sum" Management?

The implication of a command-and-control management philosophy is that whatever control or ownership is ceded to employees or customers is lost by management—that it is zero sum in nature. This is the exact opposite of the ownership state of mind, which seeks to unleash employees and customers to improve and grow a business. But it takes a certain amount of self-confidence for a manager to function in an organization with an ownership state of mind. Ownership-oriented companies like Google, for example, abide by the following principles.

- Reporting relationships are less important than the development of lines of communication running in all directions.

- There is a strong reliance on individual initiative below the management level.

- Individuals are hired for their ability to thrive on having the latitude to change the way they do their jobs, and even where and with whom they work.

How Much and What Kind of Ownership?

Ownership without limits can lead to anarchy and chaos in an organization. Therefore, as you contemplate increasing your employee and customer OQ, it's important to ask what form those limits should take. In part, the answer may depend on your context.

How Much Employee Ownership? As you've seen earlier in this book, organizations such as Baptist Health Care can achieve stunningly successful outcomes when management and employees share an ownership state of mind. BHC managers helped turn the organization around by focusing on four key characteristics: open communication, no secrets, no excuses, and ownership behavior from everyone. Management gains trust by setting the example and reflecting BHC's values in every activity. Employees respond by taking responsibility for things, such as general housekeeping, that may be outside their formal job descriptions. As the enthusiasm for this mode of management has grown across the organization, employee participation in its Bright Ideas program, for example, has resulted in more than twenty-five thousand employee suggestions being implemented over five years.

Employee ownership cultures have a tendency to produce high levels of loyalty to the organization. They also produce the occasional zealot whose pride turns to arrogance in the presence of customers. When confronted with a choice, this employee not only favors the organization over the customer but also jumps to the assumption that the customer is wrong. If the person is working within a team of employee owners, however, chances are that the problem will self-correct over time. But the risk of alienating customers is present.

Latitude to act on behalf of the customer is a hallmark of a high-ownership culture. But as you saw earlier, expanding latitude (within limits) must be preceded by hiring practices that seek out potential employees who have the right set of attitudes; you must then orient them to the values of the organization, train them carefully for the skills needed on the job, and build outstanding support systems to help them make the right decisions in a timely way. Google may hire the brightest people and the best problem solvers, but if those individuals don't work in teams or don't allow others to build on their ideas, there is probably only a limited future for them in the organization.

How Much Customer Ownership? To what degree should business functions such as sales and new product development be delegated to customers? Are there limits to the benefits of customer ownership?

Customer ownership is a mind-set foreign to many managers, but those who understand it well can build a high level of mutual loyalty and trust between customers and the organization. As with employee owners, this process begins with the careful selection of target customers. Many organizations fail to recognize that even ideal customers need training so that they can enjoy the full value the company has to offer them.

Many Silicon Valley firms enlist communities of current and potential customers to help them develop and test new products, and even sell them to others. Similarly, young entrepreneurs not steeped in traditional management concepts often turn over to their customers the responsibility for such things as sales and new product development. Karmaloop, the edgy urban apparel start-up profiled in chapter 4, offers a simple illustration.

One key decision is whether and when to give employees the authority to fire customers. This is especially important when frontline employees have direct contact with customers who can affect long-term organization morale if they fail to appreciate the overall value vision. Rarely do individuals have the authority to fire a customer. Instead, nearly all the outstanding service organizations we studied place these exceptional decisions with the teams of individuals who are best situated to evaluate whether the company would benefit by disengaging from a customer. But again, this kind of authority goes only to teams whose members have met the standards for hiring, training, and experience on the job.

What Kind of Measurement, Recognition, and Rewards?

We've defined the customer ownership quotient as the proportion of total customers who have recommended a product, service, or brand to a friend or have offered suggestions for improvements in product or service offerings and the way they are delivered. The equivalent measure for employees is the proportion of employees who have recommended the organization to a friend as a place to work or supplied suggestions for product, service, or process improvements.

Although it's important to use some variation of these metrics, we're not dogmatic about the specific formula you devise. For example, a perfectly good measure of one aspect of employee ownership is the proportion of new hires that results from employee referrals. A useful measure of the impact of employee and customer ownership is the proportion of revenue represented by employee- or customer-proposed products or services that didn't exist five years earlier. Whatever measures you choose, it is important to institutionalize them and incorporate them into your performance evaluation and reward systems, the very DNA of your organization.

With this in mind, let's review the kinds of efforts that have been put forth to track attitudes and behaviors that reflect some form of ownership.

Define Metrics for Each Level in the Ownership Hierarchy

The measurement of employee and customer relations has changed over time to reflect new research findings, new management philosophies such as customer relationship management, and new ways of interacting with employees and customers. These changes have produced an increasingly sophisticated set of metrics for the ownership hierarchy pyramid introduced in chapter 1. They are shown in Figure 8-1.

These metrics can help you steer your organization toward the top of the ownership pyramid. Along the way, you'll probably move beyond typical brand awareness and customer satisfaction ratings to measure various levels of loyalty, commitment or engagement, and finally ownership. And chances are that the closer you get to measuring a true OQ for employees as well as customers, the better you'll be able to predict financial success. Several of the metrics deserve special attention.

Satisfaction. This is perhaps the most widely used measure of employee and customer attitudes. However, research suggests a somewhat tenuous relationship between customer satisfaction and financial success, perhaps because of several factors, the most important of which is the way the measure is used. It's often associated with a question such as, "Rate your satisfaction with (your job) (our product) (our service) (your experience) on (say) a five-point scale." The results of such

FIGURE 8-1

Measurement in the employee and customer ownership quotient

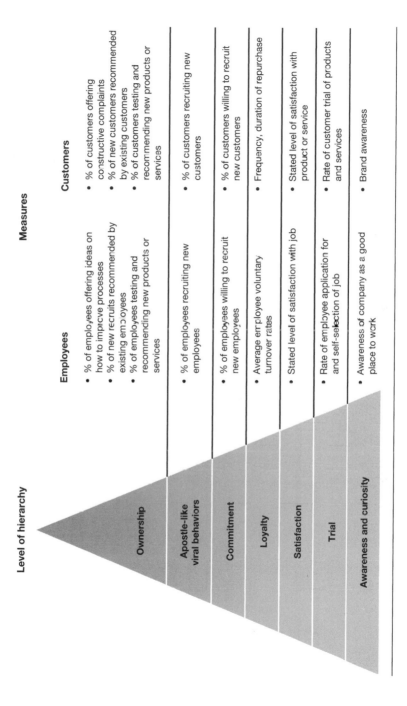

Level of hierarchy

Measures

Employees

- % of employees offering ideas on how to improve processes
- % of new recruits recommended by existing employees
- % of employees testing and recommending new products or services

- % of employees recruiting new employees

- % of employees willing to recruit new employees

- Average employee voluntary turnover rates

- Stated level of satisfaction with job

- Rate of employee application for and self-selection of job

- Awareness of company as a good place to work

Customers

- % of customers offering constructive complaints
- % of new customers recommended by existing customers
- % of customers testing and recommending new products or services

- % of customers recruiting new customers

- % of customers willing to recruit new customers

- Frequency, duration of repurchase

- Stated level of satisfaction with product or service

- Rate of customer trial of products and services

- Brand awareness

Ownership

Apostle-like viral behaviors

Commitment

Loyalty

Satisfaction

Trial

Awareness and curiosity

measures often are distorted by attempts to relate all above-average responses to, say, revenue growth or profitability.

Why? First, customers who provide anything less than top-box responses have been found to have little added inclination to repurchase, particularly in the face of lower-priced alternatives. We like to think of these responses on a five-point scale as "courtesy 4's" (where 5 is the top score). People often give courtesy 4's so as not to embarrass anyone or provoke follow-up questions. And yet organizations measuring customer satisfaction continue to reward employees for achieving favorable scores below the top-box level, further encouraging employee behaviors that have little relationship to either ownership or financial success.

Second, there may be real reasons that customer satisfaction is not related to profitability, particularly if high customer satisfaction is achieved at great expense. One of the most extreme examples of this phenomenon was probably Kozmo.com, Inc., a 1998 start-up that raised more than $100 million in venture capital. It delighted its customers by delivering an evening's entertainment (take-out food, videos, and so on—and in the case of one of our colleagues, two AA batteries for his TV remote) to customers' residences at prices comparable to those in local retail stores. Word of mouth traveled quickly about Kozmo's great service and even better prices. Revenues exploded. But the truth became clear with Kozmo's quick demise. It had been selling ten-dollar bills for five dollars.

Loyalty. Customer loyalty, which is defined in terms relevant to each organization, can have a significant impact on financial results. Loyal customers have been found to require lower marketing expenditures and lower operating costs for the marketer as a result of their educated purchasing behavior. In short, they've been trained. For example, customers of EasyJet, a European low-fare air carrier, are quite comfortable booking on the Internet and otherwise conducting themselves in ways that save money for the airline. Further, even though loyal customers expect the best prices for existing products, they are less price sensitive to new product offerings. And to the extent that they are willing to provide referrals of new customers, they can have a large impact on profitability.

Commitment or Engagement. Enterprises have been built on commitment, the willingness of customers to recommend a company or its products to others. At Intuit, for example, the early success of its personal financial software product, Quicken, was based on favorable word of mouth. Dedication to preserving customer commitment helps explain why Intuit was, and continues to be, one of the few companies to compete successfully with Microsoft.

The importance of referrals to performance has prompted new calls for asking "the ultimate question," to quote the title of a book proposing a simple, but supposedly effective, way of measuring commitment, the next level in our hierarchy.[8] The ultimate commitment question, when put to customers, is, "How willing would you be to recommend (our product) (our brand) to a (valued friend) (close relative)?" For employees (as shown earlier in figure 8-1), it is altered to, "How willing would you be to recommend our company as a place to work to a good friend?" Companies that use this metric usually tabulate the responses on a scale of 0 to 10 and subtract the percentage of 0 to 6 (low) ratings from the percentage of 9s and 10s (the highest ratings) to produce a net promoter score.

Some detractors have claimed that the net promoter score is no more effective in predicting financial success than measures of customer satisfaction. Nevertheless, an increasing number of organizations consider it a simple, useful measure of customer and employee commitment. Many also employ services that search blog sites, newsgroups, and other Internet sources for favorable and unfavorable mentions of them and their products. But eventually, the metrics of ownership will eclipse even the net promoter score in organizations that are willing to make the effort to measure them.

Ownership. Owners not only exhibit all the other behaviors in the hierarchy but also take a proprietary interest in a company, brand, or product. This means that they serve as apostles who attract new employees and customers to an organization. Among employees, this can mean increasing the number of suggestions they offer for ways of improving processes or products. For customers, it may mean everything from distributing new product samples to making repeated suggestions for new or improved products and services.

Ownership is especially prevalent in B2B businesses, where successful outcomes often require close cooperation between providers and their customers. When customers consider the product or service important to their own success, they are usually more than willing to help improve the "joint business" operation.

The ability to maintain the loyalty of customers and get their input as owners is an important element of the strategic value vision at SAS. "We invest more than 20 percent of revenues into R&D each year," says CEO James Goodnight.[9] "We even let customers vote each fall. Technical support collects suggestions from users throughout the year, and then we put it on a ballot and let all of our customers vote on the features they'd like to see added. And that becomes one of the main driving forces of R&D." More than 75 percent of the company's revenue comes from annual subscription contracts with the current customer base. Goodnight explains, "The reason they're happy with using the subscription model is that they know that this money goes back into R&D."

The advent of the Internet has enabled entire enterprises to be built on the concept of ownership. These include everything from the community-based encyclopedia Wikipedia to retailer Amazon.com. The challenge is to get owners to pay for services they feel they own. And once they pay, as eBay has found out, the challenge is to find and maintain the right balance between customer ownership and management control on behalf of investors. Some high-OQ organizations are actually changing the whole concept of management control, as Google has demonstrated.

There is no doubt that increasingly fast, easy, and individual communication has amplified the voice of the customer. Those who are willing and able to take advantage of this trend have created significant competitive advantage for their organizations.

BUILDING YOUR OWN OWNERSHIP QUOTIENT

Finding the right metrics for your OQ depends on the needs of your particular business. But as shown earlier in figure 8-1, you should at least try to measure whether your most satisfied, loyal, and committed employees and customers have successfully referred new employees and customers, respectively, or have offered some or all of the following:

- Constructive criticism of, and recommendations for improvements in, products or services

- Ideas for new products or services

- Commitment to work on behalf of the company by participating in a buzz network, distributing new product samples, and so on

The unduplicated total of the proportions of all customers and employees engaging in these behaviors represents your ownership quotient. The customer OQ won't be high. In our experience, a B2C organization that can turn a base of 3 or 4 percent of its customers into owners is well on its way to sustained success. For a B2B business, the critical percentage is higher. To accomplish this, you need a base of employee owners that represents at least 15 to 20 percent of all employees, but the ideal employee OQ to strive for should approach 100 percent, especially in a B2B setting.

A high employee and customer OQ may actually stimulate management responses that return big dividends for the organization. Consider one last remarkable story about how the company we introduced at the outset of the book, Rackspace Hosting, remade itself based on these ideas. Rackspace's experience also provides a summary of the major topics of the book.

To the extent possible, we'll let Rackspace's managers tell how they turned around a potentially failing company by creating a customer-centered organization, in the process fostering both customer and employee ownership.

From Rocky Beginnings to Fanatical Success at Rackspace

We wish we could say that Rackspace's success was all part of a grand strategy implemented from day one. But we can't, because the company's early years were anything but auspicious. Early on, its strategy resembled that of competitors: low cost, little personalized service. A customer calling with a problem would go through an extended automatic telephone protocol trying to get to a real person. Profits were elusive. As CEO Lanham Napier puts it, "We decided that things had to change, and that we could differentiate ourselves by providing personalized service delivered by human beings. One of our investment banker friends was shocked. He told us, 'Look, you're going to go broke. You've got to set this up where you never have to talk to your customers.' Fortunately, our competitors took his advice—but we didn't."[10]

Napier makes the decision sound easier than it was. It was, however, reinforced by the hiring of David Bryce as Rackspace's former director of customer relations. Bryce describes the early challenges this way: "[When I joined the company] we were trying to provide 24/7 support with five guys. They were really stretched. They didn't have the tools they needed . . . So in my first three weeks at Rackspace I ended up spending a lot of time on the phone with upset customers . . . I was tired of us letting customers down and tired of spending my time talking to customers who were justifiably upset."

Napier and CEO Graham Weston heeded Bryce's wake-up call by rethinking the business. The two men decided to change the strategic direction of the firm from equipment rental and technical support to solutions and service, and they asked Bryce to think about how to make the change. Bryce says that he realized from the outset that he had to start by turning Rackspace employees into customer fanatics:

I locked myself in the office for two days, and I wrote a twenty-page manifesto on delivering exceptional customer support, and came up with ten rules for customer fanatics. They seemed to fit the zany culture that was already developing. Out of this emerged our six core values: Fanatical Support in all we do, results first, embrace change, passion for our work, keep our promises, and treat fellow Rackers like friends and family. One key behavior associated with these values is "full disclosure: bad news first" among employees as well as between Racker teams and their customers. It is critical to fostering trust.

For Bryce's rules, see "Ten Rules for 'Fanatics' at Rackspace Hosting."

At first, Bryce's ideas about customer service caused Rackers to roll their eyes. But management put up a banner that read, "Rackspace Provides Fanatical Support." As Weston tells it, "After people stopped laughing at us, over time we kept pounding on it, pounding on it, pounding on it, and basically built it from a slogan into a real strategy."

Management did much more than create rules and slogans to engineer ownership among employees and customers. It reorganized the front line into teams of fourteen to twenty Rackers with a full range of skills and functional duties to provide 24/7 support for a designated group of customers. With team members located together in their own shared space, the mantra became, "Don't transfer the call, pass the phone." Racker teams began to exchange ideas and learn from each other as they listened in on each other's phone conversations and worked together to deliver service for their customers, a set of behaviors that is known today as Fanatical Support.

Further, management gave each team responsibility for building Rackspace's business with its customers, and rewarded the teams accordingly. This has resulted in increased business growth rates, increased Racker productivity—and increased profitability, even though Rackspace's prices can be more than an average of 10 percent over some of its competitors.

Ten Rules for "Fanatics" at Rackspace Hosting

1. Always put the customer first. Their satisfaction is of utmost importance because without them Rackspace does not exist.

2. Quality is defined by each individual customer.

3. Be reliable. Do what we said we were going to do. Keep the service promise.

4. Look for ways to exceed the customer's expectations, to surprise them, to make them say "Wow!"

5. Apologize. Fix the problem. Now.

6. The customer isn't always right. But who's right and who's wrong is irrelevant. What's important is that the customer continues to be a customer.

7. No news is not good news. Solicit feedback from customers and listen— really listen.

8. The customer's perception may be subjective, but it is still very real. Everything matters.

9. Less is more. Remove the hassle. Make it as easy as possible for our customers to do business with Rackspace.

10. Great service is a team effort.

Source: Unpublished material from Rackspace company files.

The pricing premium has not only helped pay for industry-leading service but also helps sort out those customers who truly value the exchange of ideas with frontline employees, an exchange that increasingly characterizes the company's service. Only a few customers left after the price hike—a self-selection mechanism that helped the company sharpen its target market focus. Those who remained actually increased their business with the company, becoming part of a dialogue among the members of an employee-customer community of owners working on new kinds of solutions to customer problems.

Rackspace's employee profile also shifted over time, as the customer service teams embraced Racker values and joined the community of owners. Lanham Napier explains: "What this company does, we transform a bunch of lives for Rackers. I put Rackers ahead of customers, okay? And so, for me it is about, you know, what is something special that creates the coolest place in the world for Rackers to work. When we get thousands of Rackers who share our values and are aligned around Fanatical Support, there is absolutely no stopping us."

Rackspace's Fanatical Support model soon drove the company's annual growth rate up to more than 60 by 2007. This soaring rate of growth created new challenges, including the temptation to lower hiring standards. It reinforced leadership's decision to turn hiring over to front-line teams, concluding that team members are better able than top management to resist the temptation to hire warm bodies just to fill seats.

The teams maintained the emphasis on attitude, especially toward customers. Napier—using a term that might be offensive to some people but that technical experts like to apply jokingly to themselves—puts it this way: "It starts with how we select people. We select those who are technically oriented that want to serve. Because in the Kingdom of Geeks, information is power—right? And a lot of geeks don't want to share the information. Well, we're in the service business, so it's about sharing the information with customers. It's about being completely transparent."

Not everyone fits into the Racker community, according to Henry Sauer, director of Racker Engagement: "Another thing, sort of on the dark side of all this, is you've got to be willing to get rid of people that don't fit . . . people disengaging customers, creating roadblocks on their team, just not living out the values. We don't fire somebody right off the spot. We have another person you can talk to, a woman named Karla Fulton, really 'Rackspace Mom.' She absolutely is that. She's great at coaching people and helping them turn around behavior . . . So they are given a chance, but they are not given hundreds [of chances]."

The ownership community helps explain why Rackspace recruits a large percentage of its Rackers based on recommendations from existing employees—a practice that lowers its cost for talent—and why turnover is low, something that provides the continuity of relationships that translates into perceptions of great service on the part of customers. This in turn leads to more loyal customers at Rackspace—a key ingredient in a business which typically requires a little over a year to achieve profitability in a customer relationship. Loyalty contributes to the constantly increasing volume of service requested by tenured customers, who are less costly to serve as new accounts, as the new customers typically put in two to three times more support requests in the first ninety days of service. Rackspace management estimates that during its peak growth periods, it could have grown by 20 percent per year without any new customers.

Lanham Napier has calculated that today a customer/owner has a lifetime value of at least 100 times that of a casual user of the company's services. The ownership community helps explain why Rackspace is so profitable in an industry known for low margins and modest profits.

From Fanatical Success to Sustainable Growth

By 2006, so much business was coming through the door as a result of customer referrals and general word of mouth that Napier had to turn his attention to sustainable growth. As he described it to us then, "My number one top concern is to maintain the discipline on our focused growth. Our most important constraint is increasing our production capability through new Rackers. We had to make a hard decision this year . . . that's going to sound crazy. This year our bookings started to get close to [a growth rate of] 80 percent. And we decided that we just weren't that good. So we have slowed it to 60 percent, because we felt like we started to lose our . . . ability to control that process."

The ownership state of mind has changed nearly everything about Rackspace: the kind of people it hires, the way it organizes their efforts, the way it recognizes achievement, and most importantly the way it differentiates itself from its competition in what could be a commodity-like business. It has resulted in a high employee retention rate of 87 percent, with two-thirds of all new hires recommended by current Rackers.[11] Rackspace enjoyed a (high) Net Promoter Score of more than 67 percent in early 2007, and as we've seen, the company's growth potential is so great that Rackspace has to limit the annual rate of new customer bookings. It's no wonder that CEO Napier declares, "Our culture and the awesome people we have are the things I am most proud of as well as creating an environment where people get to do what they do best . . . I would say it's impossible for our competitors to copy. They'd have to start over and build it from scratch." Or at least do what Rackspace did.

But the Rackspace story doesn't end there. In fact, one final anecdote reflects the importance of customer ownership to this company's development. David Bryce told it this way:

> [We do] e-mail surveys, phone surveys . . . We actually have our customer conference this week, where we're bringing in a bunch of customers. We have focus groups . . . We go out and visit customers . . . They tell us where to go with our product offerings. They tell us where to go with our customer portal . . . So much of—like the whole—team concept came out of a call with a customer. Back in the early days, I grabbed half the people from the support team. We went into the one conference room we had. We called this random customer, put him on speakerphone. *The whole team concept came out of that conversation with that customer.*[12]

INVENTING THE FUTURE OF OWNERSHIP

A new generation of entrepreneurs understands ownership better than do its elders. Enabled by technology and social change, they are fostering employee and customer ownership in ways that will alter the face of management.

These forces will redistribute control and make command-and-control management techniques increasingly noncompetitive, even in organizations of substantial size. After all, if employees play a major role in human resource management, product development, and process improvement, and if customers contribute significantly to marketing as well as product and process development, the traditional role of the manager must change. Few functions will be managed away from the glare of employee and customer attention.

Is your organization capable of making the transition to an ownership state of mind? We have organized some questions you can use to assess your ownership capabilities in appendix B.

Because ownership can bring significant competitive advantage along with potential pitfalls, your OQ needs to be tracked as well as nurtured. We have proposed simple ways of doing both. You'll need effective listening posts for employees and customers, and ways of organizing and acting on the information you uncover. And that's only one piece of a complex set of ideas and actions, as we have tried to show.

In short, don't think of the ownership quotient simply as a measure. Think of it as the culmination of the many decisions and activities— from philosophy and purpose to values, strategy, policies, processes, practices, and organization—that comprise an ownership state of mind. Think of it as a harbinger of the future—and if you can build an ownership state of mind for your organization, you will help create that future.

About The Service Profit Chain Institute

The Service Profit Chain Institute is a Boston-based consulting firm dedicated to helping companies achieve better performance by improving the linkages between employees, customers, and profits. It was founded by Joe Wheeler and Professors James Heskett and W. Earl Sasser Jr. of the Harvard Business School to bring the service profit chain to life in our client organizations. Our capabilities include:

- *Corporate Membership:* Visit us at serviceprofitchain.com to sign up for our online newsletter, get access to free assessment tools including the Ownership Audit and learn about becoming a corporate member of the Service Profit Chain Institute

- *Consulting Services:* Projects focused on delivering a specific aspect of the Service Profit Chain or implementation of the entire system

- *Executive Alignment:* A customized approach to working with executive teams interested in understanding the financial and organizational impact from adoption of service profit chain and

ownership quotient concepts and development of a plan for
implementation

- *Learning Systems:* Training programs and management tools
  designed to enable managers and employees to apply the proven
  practices of service profit chain leaders. Our most recent
  program, *OQ Leadership,* enables organizations to implement
  the concepts described in this book

To learn more about our capabilities, including specific tools and training to boost your organization's own *Ownership Quotient,* visit us online
at www.serviceprofitchain.com.

Auditing Ownership

This audit is intended as more than just a checklist of "must do's" to achieve a higher ownership quotient in your organization. It is designed to be used periodically to track progress in the various inputs that lead to the results reflected in the quotient itself. We have organized it in terms of, first, outputs or results—measures of performance often included in a management dashboard of indicators of progress. Next we address the most critical of the actions needed to achieve the results.

The audit can be used as is or customized by first asking respondents to identify those items that are thought to be most critical for a particular enterprise, then centering the audit on perceptions of how the organization is doing on those dimensions. Areas of greatest potential improvement are those in which perceived performance lags perceived importance the most.

Other areas of opportunity are suggested by items for which a high proportion of "don't knows" is registered. These may suggest shortcomings in measurement or the dissemination of results of measures already in place. Our experience is that in organizations with high ownership quotients, measures of performance are widely disseminated and used as the basis for best practice improvement efforts at all levels in the organization. To complete the Ownership Audit online please visit us at ownershipquotient.com or serviceprofitchain.com. Once you complete the online self-assessment version of the survey, you will be able to compare your responses to all of the respondents in our database.

THE OWNERSHIP AUDIT

If the audit is to be used as is to track trends in the measures suggested below, use the scale provided to indicate the degree to which you agree with each statement. If the audit is to be customized to reflect the priorities of a particular organization, then once respondents reach the "Input" sections of the audit, they should also fill in the circle below the number that reflects the degree of importance of that particular item.

Then respondents complete each item as described at the outset of the instructions. Once an average is calculated for the responses on the importance scale and the performance scale, the latter should be subtracted from the former to calculate the "performance gap" on each item between importance and actual performance. Positive numbers on the performance gap suggest that little improvement may be needed. Negative numbers suggest priorities for further improvement.

Section 1
OUTPUTS OR RESULTS: EMPLOYEES

For each item below, rate the degree to which you *agree* that this practice is true for your organization by marking the appropriate number.

Scoring range (Agreement): 0 = Don't know; 1 = Strongly disagree; 5 = Neither agree nor disagree; 9 = Strongly agree

Item	*Agreement*
1. Our employee retention level is high for our industry.	0 1 2 3 4 5 6 7 8 9 ○○○○○○○○○○
2. Our employee productivity is high for our industry.	0 1 2 3 4 5 6 7 8 9 ○○○○○○○○○○

3. Our proportion of (new hires) (job applicants) resulting from employee referrals is high for our industry.	0 1 2 3 4 5 6 7 8 9 ○○○○○○○○○○
4. Our number of employee suggestions for product or process improvement is high for our industry.	0 1 2 3 4 5 6 7 8 9 ○○○○○○○○○○

Section 2
OUTPUTS OR RESULTS: CUSTOMERS

For each item below, rate the degree to which you *agree* that this practice is true for your organization by marking the appropriate number.

Scoring range (Agreement): 0 = Don't know; 1 = Strongly disagree; 5 = Neither agree nor disagree; 9 = Strongly agree

Item	Agreement
5. Our customer retention rates are high for our industry.	0 1 2 3 4 5 6 7 8 9 ○○○○○○○○○○
6. Our share of the total expenditures for the products we sell and the services we deliver are high for our industry.	0 1 2 3 4 5 6 7 8 9 ○○○○○○○○○○
7. Our proportion of new customers referred by existing ones is high for our industry.	0 1 2 3 4 5 6 7 8 9 ○○○○○○○○○○
8. Our number of customer suggestions for product or process improvements is high for our industry.	0 1 2 3 4 5 6 7 8 9 ○○○○○○○○○○

Section 3
OUTPUTS OR RESULTS: FINANCIAL

For each item below, rate the degree to which you *agree* that this practice is true for your organization by marking the appropriate number.

Scoring range (Agreement): 0 = Don't know; 1 = Strongly disagree; 5 = Neither agree nor disagree; 9 = Strongly agree

Item	Agreement
9. Our rate of sales increase is high for our industry.	0 1 2 3 4 5 6 7 8 9
10. Our rate of profit on sales is high for our industry.	0 1 2 3 4 5 6 7 8 9

Section 4

INPUTS: BUILD OWNERSHIP INTO YOUR STRATEGIC VALUE VISION

For each item below, rate the degree to which you *agree* that this practice is true for your organization. Then rate its level of *importance* to your organization's success.

Scoring range (Agreement): 0 = Don't know; 1 = Strongly disagree; 5 = Neither agree nor disagree; 9 = Strongly agree

Scoring range (Importance): 0 = Don't know; 1 = Not at all important; 5 = Moderate importance; 9 = Great importance

Item	Agreement	Importance
11. My organization has clearly defined the customers it seeks and does not seek to serve.	0 1 2 3 4 5 6 7 8 9	0 1 2 3 4 5 6 7 8 9
12. Our business is defined in terms of value (results and quality of experience) rather than products and services desired by targeted customers.	0 1 2 3 4 5 6 7 8 9	0 1 2 3 4 5 6 7 8 9
13. We clearly define value for both targeted customers and targeted employees.	0 1 2 3 4 5 6 7 8 9	0 1 2 3 4 5 6 7 8 9
14. Our policies, organization, performance measures, and compensation are internally consistent and designed to deliver maximum difference between value and cost.	0 1 2 3 4 5 6 7 8 9	0 1 2 3 4 5 6 7 8 9

15. Support systems (including information systems, networks, locations, and facility designs) are designed to provide maximum support to our operating strategy.	0 1 2 3 4 5 6 7 8 9 ○○○○○○○○○○	0 1 2 3 4 5 6 7 8 9 ○○○○○○○○○○

Section 5

INPUTS: LEVER VALUE OVER COSTS

For each item below, rate the degree to which you *agree* that this practice is true for your organization. Then rate its level of *importance* to your organization's success.

Scoring range (Agreement): 0 = Don't know; 1 = Strongly disagree; 5 = Neither agree nor disagree; 9 = Strongly agree

Scoring range (Importance): 0 = Don't know; 1 = Not at all important; 5 = Moderate importance; 9 = Great importance

Item	*Agreement*	*Importance*
16. Our organization has defined its customer value equation clearly and communicated it widely.	0 1 2 3 4 5 6 7 8 9 ○○○○○○○○○○	0 1 2 3 4 5 6 7 8 9 ○○○○○○○○○○
17. Our organization creates operating leverage through the design of the customer experience.	0 1 2 3 4 5 6 7 8 9 ○○○○○○○○○○	0 1 2 3 4 5 6 7 8 9 ○○○○○○○○○○
18. We understand, measure, and communicate performance on the "deep indicators" in our business.	0 1 2 3 4 5 6 7 8 9 ○○○○○○○○○○	0 1 2 3 4 5 6 7 8 9 ○○○○○○○○○○
19. Individual unit performance is tracked and compared with other units; unit managers are encouraged to consult with peers to observe and transfer best practice.	0 1 2 3 4 5 6 7 8 9 ○○○○○○○○○○	0 1 2 3 4 5 6 7 8 9 ○○○○○○○○○○

Section 6
INPUTS: PUT CUSTOMERS TO WORK

For each item below, rate the degree to which you *agree* that this practice is true for your organization. Then rate its level of *importance* to your organization's success.

Scoring range (Agreement): 0 = Don't know; 1 = Strongly disagree; 5 = Neither agree nor disagree; 9 = Strongly agree

Scoring range (Importance): 0 = Don't know; 1 = Not at all important; 5 = Moderate importance; 9 = Great importance

Item	Agreement	Importance
20. Our organization has clear objectives for putting customers to work.	0 1 2 3 4 5 6 7 8 9 ○○○○○○○○○○	0 1 2 3 4 5 6 7 8 9 ○○○○○○○○○○
21. We have designed ways of engaging customers in sales by means of an effective customer referral process.	0 1 2 3 4 5 6 7 8 9 ○○○○○○○○○○	0 1 2 3 4 5 6 7 8 9 ○○○○○○○○○○
22. We engage customers in delivering their own services where this improves quality and reduces cost.	0 1 2 3 4 5 6 7 8 9 ○○○○○○○○○○	0 1 2 3 4 5 6 7 8 9 ○○○○○○○○○○
23. We apply processes or technology that make it easy for customers to interact with our company.	0 1 2 3 4 5 6 7 8 9 ○○○○○○○○○○	0 1 2 3 4 5 6 7 8 9 ○○○○○○○○○○
24. We have methods in place for listening, measuring, and responding to the customer's voice.	0 1 2 3 4 5 6 7 8 9 ○○○○○○○○○○	0 1 2 3 4 5 6 7 8 9 ○○○○○○○○○○
25. In designing processes for putting customers to work, our organization constantly takes the customer's point of view.	0 1 2 3 4 5 6 7 8 9 ○○○○○○○○○○	0 1 2 3 4 5 6 7 8 9 ○○○○○○○○○○

Section 7

INPUTS: BOOST YOUR EMPLOYEE OQ

For each item below, rate the degree to which you *agree* that this practice is true for your organization. Then rate its level of *importance* to your organization's success.

Scoring range (Agreement): 0 = Don't know; 1 = Strongly disagree; 5 = Neither agree nor disagree; 9 = Strongly agree

Scoring range (Importance): 0 = Don't know; 1 = Not at all important; 5 = Moderate importance; 9 = Great importance

Item	Agreement	Importance
26. We have made an effort to define the elements of the employee value equation in our organization.	0 1 2 3 4 5 6 7 8 9	0 1 2 3 4 5 6 7 8 9
27. We hire primarily for attitude.	0 1 2 3 4 5 6 7 8 9	0 1 2 3 4 5 6 7 8 9
28. We provide realistic job previews.	0 1 2 3 4 5 6 7 8 9	0 1 2 3 4 5 6 7 8 9
29. We train primarily for skills and broader personal development.	0 1 2 3 4 5 6 7 8 9	0 1 2 3 4 5 6 7 8 9
30. We offer employees wide latitude (within limits) to deliver value to targeted customers.	0 1 2 3 4 5 6 7 8 9	0 1 2 3 4 5 6 7 8 9
31. We measure, reward, and recognize those who use their latitude to deliver results to others.	0 1 2 3 4 5 6 7 8 9	0 1 2 3 4 5 6 7 8 9
32. Employees are encouraged to suggest new products and processes and are recognized for it.	0 1 2 3 4 5 6 7 8 9	0 1 2 3 4 5 6 7 8 9
33. Employees are encouraged to refer potential job candidates and are recognized for it.	0 1 2 3 4 5 6 7 8 9	0 1 2 3 4 5 6 7 8 9

34. We train customers in what to expect to facilitate employee service delivery.	0 1 2 3 4 5 6 7 8 9 ○○○○○○○○○○	0 1 2 3 4 5 6 7 8 9 ○○○○○○○○○○

Section 8

INPUTS: ENGINEER OWNERSHIP THROUGH ANTICIPATORY MANAGEMENT

For each item below, rate the degree to which you *agree* that this practice is true for your organization. Then rate its level of *importance* to your organization's success.

Scoring range (Agreement): 0 = Don't know; 1 = Strongly disagree; 5 = Neither agree nor disagree; 9 = Strongly agree

Scoring range (Importance): 0 = Don't know; 1 = Not at all important; 5 = Moderate importance; 9 = Great importance

Item	Agreement	Importance
35. Where possible, we seek to develop a community of customers who accept ownership responsibilities.	0 1 2 3 4 5 6 7 8 9 ○○○○○○○○○○	0 1 2 3 4 5 6 7 8 9 ○○○○○○○○○○
36. Functions in our organization share a common customer preferences database.	0 1 2 3 4 5 6 7 8 9 ○○○○○○○○○○	0 1 2 3 4 5 6 7 8 9 ○○○○○○○○○○
37. We have developed technology and processes to predict and act upon customer needs and behaviors in an effort to consistently exceed their expectations.	0 1 2 3 4 5 6 7 8 9 ○○○○○○○○○○	0 1 2 3 4 5 6 7 8 9 ○○○○○○○○○○
38. Operations, marketing, and human resources are coordinated to act on predictive intelligence about customer preferences or needs.	0 1 2 3 4 5 6 7 8 9 ○○○○○○○○○○	0 1 2 3 4 5 6 7 8 9 ○○○○○○○○○○

Section 9

INPUTS: BUILD A STRONG AND ADAPTIVE OWNERSHIP CULTURE

For each item below, rate the degree to which you *agree* that this practice is true for your organization. Then rate its level of *importance* to your organization's success.

Scoring range (Agreement): 0 = Don't know; 1 = Strongly disagree; 5 = Neither agree nor disagree; 9 = Strongly agree

Scoring range (Importance): 0 = Don't know; 1 = Not at all important; 5 = Moderate importance; 9 = Great importance

Item	*Agreement*	*Importance*
39. Our organization has identified the core values and behaviors that continue to contribute to its success.	0 1 2 3 4 5 6 7 8 9 ○○○○○○○○○○	0 1 2 3 4 5 6 7 8 9 ○○○○○○○○○○
40. Behaviors are observed and measured to insure that they conform to the values.	0 1 2 3 4 5 6 7 8 9 ○○○○○○○○○○	0 1 2 3 4 5 6 7 8 9 ○○○○○○○○○○
41. Regardless of performance, managers not able to exhibit behaviors desired by the organization are subject to training and, if necessary, dismissal.	0 1 2 3 4 5 6 7 8 9 ○○○○○○○○○○	0 1 2 3 4 5 6 7 8 9 ○○○○○○○○○○
42. Our organization has a strong sense of shared purpose.	0 1 2 3 4 5 6 7 8 9 ○○○○○○○○○○	0 1 2 3 4 5 6 7 8 9 ○○○○○○○○○○
43. Our leaders use story telling and other tools as means for preserving and evolving our company culture.	0 1 2 3 4 5 6 7 8 9 ○○○○○○○○○○	0 1 2 3 4 5 6 7 8 9 ○○○○○○○○○○

Section 10
INPUTS: SUSTAIN YOUR SUCCESS

For each item below, rate the degree to which you *agree* that this practice is true for your organization. Then rate its level of *importance* to your organization's success.

Scoring range (Agreement): 0 = Don't know; 1 = Strongly disagree; 5 = Neither agree nor disagree; 9 = Strongly agree

Scoring range (Importance): 0 = Don't know; 1 = Not at all important; 5 = Moderate importance; 9 = Great importance

Item	Agreement	Importance
44. Management makes an effort to establish an "ownership state of mind" among employees in this organization.	0 1 2 3 4 5 6 7 8 9 ○○○○○○○○○○	0 1 2 3 4 5 6 7 8 9 ○○○○○○○○○○
45. To the extent possible, teams are employed at the customer contact level.	0 1 2 3 4 5 6 7 8 9 ○○○○○○○○○○	0 1 2 3 4 5 6 7 8 9 ○○○○○○○○○○
46. Employees play a significant role in the selection, training, and provision of peer pressure for new hires with whom they will be working.	0 1 2 3 4 5 6 7 8 9 ○○○○○○○○○○	0 1 2 3 4 5 6 7 8 9 ○○○○○○○○○○
47. There is a strong reliance on individual initiative below the management level.	0 1 2 3 4 5 6 7 8 9 ○○○○○○○○○○	0 1 2 3 4 5 6 7 8 9 ○○○○○○○○○○
48. Individuals are hired in part for their ability to thrive on latitude to change the way they do their jobs.	0 1 2 3 4 5 6 7 8 9 ○○○○○○○○○○	0 1 2 3 4 5 6 7 8 9 ○○○○○○○○○○

49. Efforts are made to identify, develop, and measure customer ownership behaviors such as referrals of new customers and suggestions for product or process improvements.	0 1 2 3 4 5 6 7 8 9 ○ ○ ○ ○ ○ ○ ○ ○ ○ ○	0 1 2 3 4 5 6 7 8 9 ○ ○ ○ ○ ○ ○ ○ ○ ○ ○
50. Efforts are made to identify, develop, and measure employee ownership behaviors such as referrals of new potential employees and suggestions for product or process improvements.	0 1 2 3 4 5 6 7 8 9 ○ ○ ○ ○ ○ ○ ○ ○ ○ ○	0 1 2 3 4 5 6 7 8 9 ○ ○ ○ ○ ○ ○ ○ ○ ○ ○

ACKNOWLEDGMENTS

This book has had a long gestation period. In a sense, it has been more than thirty years in the making. More immediately, it has required more than two years of intense effort. As a result, we have accumulated debts to a number of people.

First and foremost, we have had the cooperation of a number of executives in the firms that we have studied in some depth. They include:

Baptist Health Care: Robert Johnson, Dr. David DiLoreto, Ava Abney, Celeste Norris, Sherry Harnett, Al Stubblefield, Diane Wilbanks, Bob Harriman

Build-A-Bear Workshop®: Darlene Elder, Scott Seay, Scott Gower, Michelle LeMoine, Teresa Kroll, Maxine Clark

EMC: Frank Hauck, Leo Colborne, Stacey Yeoman, Polly Pearson, Jim Bampos

Fairmont Hotels & Resorts: Jeff Senior, Carolyn Clark, Chris Cahill, Brian Richardson, Jon Mamela, Ian Wilson, Tom Story

Harrah's Entertainment: David Norton, John Bruns, Mary Thomas, Terry Byrnes, John Baker, Wade Faul, John Koster, Stephanie Winslow, Fernando Ramirez, George Dittmann, Reggie Kirk, Kathy Mayor

ING Direct: Arkadi Kuhlmann

Irving Oil: Al Bugby, Cate Rafferty, Harry Hadiaris, Lou Beam, Doug Sanders, Leon Jessman, Ben Bolen, Marney Shoring, Tim Guen, Mike Crosby, Kathryn Barnicle

Mo's–A Place for Steaks: Johnny Vassallo

Limited Brands: Leslie Wexner, Sharen Turney

PrairieStone Pharmacy: John Brady, Cheri Morris, Ken Henjum

Rackspace Hosting: Henry Sauer, David Bryce, Lanham Napier, Graham Weston, Halli Holliman, Stacy Marshall

SAS: Dr. James Goodnight, Annette Harris, Beverly Brown, Pamela Meek, Suzanne Gordon, Jenn Mann, Jim Davis

Wegmans Food Markets: Danny Wegman, Karen Shadders, Jack DePeters, Mary Ellen Burris, Jo Natale

Included among these are our former colleagues Gary Loveman and Len Schlesinger, who left academe to successfully put these ideas, among others, into practice in the real world.

As has been the case for years, we are also indebted to others of our current and former colleagues who continue to examine topics related to the service profit chain and the ownership quotient. They include Jeffrey Rayport, David Maister, Tom Jones, Roger Hallowell, Frances Frei, Ashish Anand, Das Narayandas, Jim Cash, Luis Huete, Tom Eisenmann, and Tom DeLong.

We owe a real debt to the people whose practices continue to stimulate our thinking and ideas and provide the grist for our field research. Most recently, they include: CEO Andy Fromm and his colleagues at the Service Management Group, whose extensive database regarding service profit chain relationships they have shared with us from time to time; Diane Hessan, CEO of Communispace; and Pete Blackshaw, executive vice president, Nielsen Online Digital Strategic Services.

The research team from The Service Profit Chain Institute provided us with insightful and thorough qualitative and quantitative analysis. They include Dr. Maria Broderick, Brian Goodman, Vickie Pittard, Stephanie Korney, Cynthia Jacobs, James Esposito, and Gaurav Chauhan and the research team at RocSearch in India.

At HBS Press, Astrid Sandoval, Hollis Heimbouch, Jacque Murphy, David Goehring, Carolyn Monaco, Stephani Finks, and Ania Wieckowski were particularly helpful in both soliciting feedback from others and providing their expert opinions that helped us position our work more effectively, and we are grateful to Colleen Kaftan for her superb editing.

And finally, we are indebted to our spouses, Marilyn Heskett, Connie Sasser, and Laura Gallant as they patiently awaited the completion of the book with the full knowledge that the work behind it will continue.

NOTES

Chapter 1

1. See, for example, David H. Maister, *Practice What You Preach: What Managers Must Do to Create a High Achievement Culture* (New York: The Free Press, 2001).

2. Jan Carlson, *Moments of Truth* (Cambridge, MA: Ballinger Publishing Company, 1987).

3. Carolyn Clark, Fairmont Hotels & Resorts 2008 HR Conference Presentation.

4. Interview with Carolyn Clark, November 2006, Toronto.

5. Ibid.

6. As measured by net promoter score as well as other measures. Introduced in a 2003 article in *Harvard Business Review*, the concept is discussed at length in Fred Reichheld, *The Ultimate Question: Driving Good Profits and True Growth* (Boston: Harvard Business School Publishing, 2006). To calculate the net promoter score, you take the responses, on a scale of 1 to 10, to the question, "How likely is it that you would recommend us to a friend or colleague?" You subtract the percentage of 0–6 scores from the percentage of 9 and 10 scores to produce the net promoter score.

Chapter 2

1. The descriptions in this section are based on James L. Heskett, "ING Direct," Case 9-804-167 (Boston: Harvard Business School Publishing, February 1, 2005).

2. Stanley Reed, Diane Brady, and Bruce Einhorn, "Rolls-Royce At Your Service," *BusinessWeek*, November 14, 2005, 92–95.

3. Kerry Capell, "IKEA: How the Swedish Retailer Became a Global Cult Brand," *BusinessWeek*, November 14, 2005, 97–106.

4. John Case, "Customer Service: The Last Word," *Inc. Magazine*, April 1991, 1–5.

5. Clayton M. Christensen and Michael E. Raynor, *The Innovator's Solution: Creating and Sustaining Successful Growth* (Boston: Harvard Business School Press, 2003), 74.

6. Ibid., 74–75.

7. Theodore Levitt, "Marketing Myopia," *Harvard Business Review*, July–August 1960, 45.

8. Peter Drucker, *The Essential Drucker* (New York: Harper Collins, 2001), 24–25.

9. Michael Cusumano, "The Changing Software Business: Moving from Products to Services," *Computer*, vol 41, no 1, January 2008.

10. Steve Hamm and Spencer E. Ante, "Beyond Blue," *BusinessWeek*, April 18, 2005, 67.

11. This quotation and the material in this example are based on "How to Break Out of Commodity Hell," *BusinessWeek*, March 27, 2006, 76.

Chapter 3

1. *Enhancing Prescription Medicine Adherence: A National Action Plan*, National Council on Patient Information and Education, August 2007, 3.

2. Based on interviews with PrairieStone pharmacy managers, March 2006.

3. "2005 Pharmacy Chain of the Year," *Drug Topics*, April 18, 2005, 52, 54, and 56.

4. New York Police Department, "Report of Crime Trends in Major U.S. Cities: Total Crime Index for 29 Largest Cities."

5. Interview between William Bratton and one of the authors, New York, February 1994.

6. Information about Victoria's Secret is based on interviews with the company's management between 2005 and 2008. One of the authors is a director of the company's parent, Limited Brands.

7. Interview with Darlene Elder, February 2007.

Chapter 4

1. As quoted in Pete Blackshaw, "The Six Drivers of Brand Credibility," *Customer Relationship Management*, September 2007, 21–25.

2. Interview with Diane Hessan, April 26, 2007.

3. John H. Fleming and Jim Asplund, *Human Sigma* (New York: Gallup Press, 2007), 87–98.

4. As you will see in chapter 7, Irving Oil, a retailer of petroleum and other products, had to overcome this negative attitude to deliver its strategic value vision of building customer loyalty based on interactions with its employees.

5. James L. Heskett, Shouldice Hospital Limited, Case no. 9-683-068 (Boston: Harvard Business School Publishing, 1983).

6. Kerry Capell, "IKEA: How the Swedish Retailer Became a Global Cult Brand," *BusinessWeek*, November 14, 2005, 97–106.

7. The first study that established this relationship was carried out years ago. See Technical Assistance Research Programs Institute, Part II, performed for the U.S. Office of Consumer Affairs, April 1, 1986, 50.

8. See, for example, Pete Blackshaw, *Satisfied Customers Tell Three Friends, Angry Customers Tell 3,000: The New Realities of Running a Business in Today's Consumer Driven World* (New York: Currency Doubleday, 2008).

9. See James L. Heskett, W. Earl Sasser, and Leonard A. Schlesinger, *The Value Profit Chain: How Leading Companies Link Profit and Growth to Loyalty, Satisfaction, and Value* (New York: The Free Press, 1997), 58–59.

10. Lands' End, http://www.landsend.com.

11. Southwest Airlines, http://www.southwest.com/help/boardingschool/faq.html.

12. Pete Blackshaw, *Satisfied Customers Tell Three Friends, Angry Customers Tell 3,000*.

13. http://www.tcho.com/.

14. Quotations from EMC executives are from interviews conducted by the authors in September 2006.

Chapter 5

1. See James L. Heskett, W. Earl Sasser, and Leonard A. Schlesinger, *The Value Profit Chain: Treat Employees Like Customers and Customers Like Employees* (New York: The Free Press, 2003). In the most comprehensive study to date of cause and effect, David H. Maister reports in his book, *Practice What You Preach: What Managers Must Do to Create a High Achievement Culture* (New York: The Free Press, 2001), that employee satisfaction is a major contributor to quality and client relationships, and ultimately to financial performance.

2. Fairmont company files, April 2007.

3. Deborah Kovacs and Jared T. Williams, *Katie Copley* (Jaffrey, NH: David R. Godine, 2007).

4. Interview with Danny Wegman, Rochester, NY, November 2006.

5. http://www.sas.com/corporate/worklife/index.html, July 2008.

6. Interview with John Brady, November 2006.

7. From videotaped interview with Scott Cook, 1992, by Tom Ryder, HBS Publishing, Boston.

8. Wegman interview.

9. Quoted in Mike McNamee, "Credit Card Revolutionary," *Stanford Business*, May 2001, 23.

10. Al Stubblefield, *The Baptist Health Care Journey to Excellence: Creating a Culture that WOWs!* (New York: John Wiley & Sons, 2005), 78.

11. "ASTD 2007 State of the Industry Report," American Society for Training and Development, 2007.

12. Tony Bingham and Pat Galagan, "A Higher Level of Learning," *T&D*, September 2005.

13. Rex Davenport, "Wegmans–A Shared Vision," *T&D*, September 2005.

14. Quotations from EMC executives are from interviews conducted by the authors in September 2006.

15. Quotations from SAS executives are from interviews conducted by the authors in November 2006.

16. This and other quotations from living managers in this chapter are based on interviews conducted by the authors in September 2006, Portsmouth, NH.

17. Frederick Herzberg, *Work and the Nature of Man* (Cleveland, OH: Word Publishing, 1966).

18. Quotations from interview with Carolyn Clark, November 2006, Toronto.

19. "Special Report: Customer Service Champs," *BusinessWeek*, March 3, 2008.

20. Steve Hamm, with Ian Rowley, "How to Break Out of Commodity Hell," *BusinessWeek*, March 27, 2006, 76.

21. Rachel Beck, "Lessons in How Circuit City's Job Cuts Backfired," *San Francisco Chronicle*, January 13, 2008, C3.

22. Bingham and Galagan, "A Higher Level of Learning."

23. Jena McGregor, "The 2008 Winners," *BusinessWeek*, March 3, 2008, 47–50.

24. John E. Hunter, Frank L. Schmidt, and Michael K. Judiesch, "Individual Differences in Output Variability as a Function of Job Complexity," *Journal of Applied Psychology* 75, no. 1 (1990): 28–42.

Chapter 6

1. "Active enterprise" described in "Harrah's Doubles Down for I.T.," *CIO Magazine*, February 1, 2003.

2. Unless otherwise indicated, all the quotations from executives and workers are from our interviews with them.

3. Rajiv Lal, "Harrah's Entertainment Inc.," Case 9-502-011 (Boston: Harvard Business School Publishing, 2002).

4. See, for example, Gail McGovern and Youngme Moon, "Companies and the Customers Who Hate Them," *Harvard Business Review*, June 2007, 78–84.

5. Victoria Chang and Jeffrey Pfeffer, "Gary Loveman and Harrah's Entertainment," Case OB-45 (Stanford, CA: Stanford Graduate School of Business, November 4, 2003).

6. Gary Loveman, "Diamonds in the Data Mine," *Harvard Business Review Reprint*, May 2003, 3.

7. Rajiv Lal, "Harrah's Entertainment Inc."

8. Chang and Pfeffer, "Gary Loveman and Harrah's Entertainment," 10.

9. "Harrah's Doubles Down for I.T.," *CIO Magazine*, February 1, 2003, 32.

Chapter 7

1. John P. Kotter and James L. Heskett, *Corporate Culture and Performance* (New York: The Free Press, 1991).

2. This and other quotations from Baptist Health Care executives not otherwise attributed in this chapter are based on interviews conducted by the authors in October and November 2006.

3. Al Stubblefield, *The Baptist Health Care Journey to Excellence* (New York: John Wiley & Sons, 2005), 5.

4. This and other quotations from Irving managers in this chapter are based on interviews conducted by the authors in September 2006.

5. This and other quotations from SAS managers in this chapter are based on interviews conducted by the authors in October 2006.

6. Stubblefield, *The Baptist Health Care Journey to Excellence*, 20.

7. Jim Collins, *Good to Great: Why Some Companies Make the Leap . . . and Others Don't* (New York: HarperCollins, 2001), 12–13.

8. Kotter and Heskett, *Corporate Culture and Performance*.

9. Stubblefield, *The Baptist Health Care Journey to Excellence*, 23.

Chapter 8

1. Tom Peters and R. H. Waterman, *In Search of Excellence* (New York: Harper & Row, 1982).

2. Gary Hamel with Bill Breen, *The Future of Management* (Boston: Harvard Business School Press, 2007), especially 101–119.

3. Justin Wolfers and Eric W. Zitzewitz, "Using Prediction Markets to Track Information Flows: Evidence from Google," a paper presented January 4, 2008, at a meeting of the American Economic Association, as reported in Noam Cohen, "Google's Lunchtime Betting Game," *New York Times*, January 7, 2008, C4.

4. Ibid.

5. "100 Best Companies to Work For, 2007," *Fortune*, January 22, 2007.

6. Quoted in Henry Tricks, "High-Tech Strengthens the Mix," *Financial Times*, November 16, 2000, 19.

7. Simon Romero, "Mexico Cement Giant Plans Internet Emphasis," *New York Times*, September 13, 2000.

8. Frederick Reichheld, *The Ultimate Question: Driving Good Profits and True Growth* (Boston: Harvard Business School Press, 2006).

9. Quotations from SAS executives are from interviews conducted by the authors in November 2006.

10. Quotations from Rackspace executives are from interviews conducted by the authors in March 2006.

11. In early 2008, Rackspace was named by *Fortune* as number 32 on its list of the 100 best places to work. It was the first time that the company had participated in the competition.

12. David Bryce, interview by the authors, February 2006.

INDEX

ABOUT THE AUTHORS

James L. Heskett is a Baker Foundation Professor Emeritus at the Harvard Business School. He completed his PhD at the Graduate School of Business, Stanford University, and has been a member of the faculty of The Ohio State University as well as President of Logistics Systems, Inc. He is currently on the faculty of several short executive programs at HBS.

He is a member of the Board of Directors of Limited Brands and has served as a consultant to companies in North America, Latin America, and Europe. He is a founding partner of The Service Profit Chain Institute.

Professor Heskett was the 1974 recipient of the John Drury Sheahan Award of the Council of Logistics Management and the 1992 Marketing Educator of the Year Award of Sales and Marketing Executives International.

Among his publications are more than a dozen books, including co-authorship of *The Value Profit Chain* (Free Press, 2003); *The Service Profit Chain* (Free Press, 1997), and *Corporate Culture and Performance* (Free Press, 1992). He has authored numerous articles in such publications as *Harvard Business Review, Journal of Marketing, Sloan Management Review, California Management Review*, and others.

A member of the faculty of the Harvard Business School since 1965, he has taught courses in marketing, business logistics, the management of service operations, business policy, service management, and general management.

W. Earl Sasser, formerly The UPS Foundation Chair of Service Management, is now a Baker Foundation Professor at Harvard Business School. He has been a member of the faculty there since 1969. He received a BA in Mathematics from Duke University in 1965, an MBA from the University of North Carolina in 1967, and a PhD in Economics from Duke University in 1969.

Professor Sasser developed the School's first course on the management of service operations in 1972. He has taught a variety of courses in the MBA program, including Production and Operations Management, Decision Making and Ethical Values, The Operating Manager, and Service Management. He currently teaches in the Program for Leadership Development, an executive education program he cofounded in 2005.

In 1982, Sasser's excellence in the classroom was recognized in a *Fortune* article profiling eight professors from business schools throughout the country. Professor Sasser was Chairman of the MBA Program from 1988 to 1991. He was also faculty chair of the Advanced Management Program executive program from 1992–1995. From 1995 to 2000 Professor Sasser served as Senior Associate Dean of Executive Education.

In 1990 he coauthored (with James L. Heskett and Christopher W. L. Hart) *Service Breakthroughs: Changing the Rules of the Game.* Based on five years of extensive research in fourteen service industries, it explains how one or two firms in each industry are constantly able to set new standards for quality and value that force competitors to adapt or fail. Sasser has coauthored several other books in the field of service management, including *Management of Service Operations* and *The Service Management Course, The Service Profit Chain,* and his latest book, *The Value Profit Chain* (with Professor James L. Heskett and Leonard A. Schlesinger; Free Press, 2003).

Sasser has written or cowritten ten articles for Harvard Business Review, including "Putting the Service Profit Chain to Work," "The

Profitable Art of Service Recovery," "Zero Defections: Quality Comes to Services," "Match Supply and Demand in Service Industries," and "Why Satisfied Customer Defect."

Professor Sasser serves as a consultant to a number of companies in North America, Asia, and Europe and is a founding partner of The Service Profit Chain Institute.

Joe Wheeler is the Executive Director of The Service Profit Chain Institute, a Boston-based consulting firm dedicated to helping companies achieve better performance by improving the linkage between employees, customers, and profits. The Service Profit Chain Institute was founded by Mr. Wheeler and James Heskett and W. Earl Sasser to partner with companies to bring the concepts associated with The Service Profit Chain to life in their own organizations.

Prior to launching The Service Profit Chain Institute, Mr. Wheeler was the Managing Director of Customer Experience for FleetBoston Financial/Bank of America, where he was responsible for customer experience, quality, and productivity. Prior to this, he was an Executive Vice President with The Forum Corporation, where he managed the firm's Customer Experience Consulting Practice and co-authored *Managing the Customer Experience—Turning Customers into Advocates* (FT Prentice-Hall, 2002).

Mr. Wheeler's client work includes strategic projects for many organizations, including Kraft General Foods, Irving Oil Ltd., Fairmont Hotels & Resorts, Manulife Financial, Export Development Corporation, Sun Life of Canada, Canadian Imperial Bank of Commerce and PayPal.

Mr. Wheeler completed his MBA at the Edinburgh Business School and studied Arts and Science at the University of Toronto and Queen's University in Kingston.